2ND EDITION-EXPANDED

The

Home Owner's Diary

Keep Important Facts About Your Home

By Della Sheffield

CONTENTS

FINANCE

EXTERIOR

INTERIOR ROOMS

HALLWAYS

BEDROOMS

UTILITIES

CONTENTS (CONTINUED)

 ## GARAGE

CLIMATE CONTROL

SECURITY

 ## WATER

 ## ADDITIONAL ROOMS

PHONE

In spite of inflation, high mortgage rates and taxes, home ownership is still the best, safest and wisest investment a family can make. But the days of high construction and repair costs are here to stay. Every homeowner knows that in order to save money, they have to keep track of what they spend for every home improvement, every appliance, and everything in their house that can break, wear out, or come up on a tax audit.

It is easy to outgrow the simple record-keeping methods that most of us begin with: the checkbook register, pocket notepad, shoebox or stuffed manila file folder. Sooner of later each of these becomes overwhelmed with the volume of records being generated by even very new homeowners. What needs to replace them is a system of recordkeeping that is dependable, expandable, comprehensive and consistent. This **Home Owner's Diary** was created for that purpose.

If you are planning to buy or build a new home, hire a building contractor, or undertake some major renovations or repairs, this book will teach you how to track your purchases and what needs to be recorded. Just as you need the proper tools and skill to bring your project to successful completion, you need the proper tools and skill to record each transaction and be able to access it easily in the future. The **Home Owner's Diary** is the tool you need to gain the skills of recordkeeping that will serve you in good stead into the indefinite future.

— *Della Sheffield*

INCOME OR CAPITAL GAIN TAX

The following is important documentation for determining possible income or capital gain taxes on the sale of your home. This is a general overview and not a comprehensive discussion of all tax aspects of buying, selling or repairing a home. You should consult your tax advisor regarding these matters.

Good records are necessary to determine the "tax basis" of your home. Your gain on sale of your home is the contract sales price less the tax basis of your home. The tax basis is the original contract price when you purchased your home, plus certain settlement charges or closing costs of purchasing, refinancing and/or selling the home, minus prior deferred gains on sale of a prior residence sold before May 7, 1997, plus improvements to your home while you owned it.

Settlement charges or closing costs incurred when purchasing, refinancing or selling your home include sales/broker commissions, attorney fees, appraisal fees, title costs, loan placement charges, and so forth. However, you cannot add certain items to the tax basis, such as fire insurance premiums, amount deposited to escrow, some mortgage insurance premiums and so forth. Generally these items are located on the Closing Statement (HUD-1) when you purchase, refinance, and/or sell your home. Keep your closing statements along with this handbook for your tax advisor.

Improvements are items that add value to your home. Examples are an upgraded heating system, storm windows, land improvements, upgraded roof, swimming pool, new kitchen and additional rooms. You should document these items, which increase your tax basis of your home. Repairs are things done to keep your home operable daily. Repairs can include painting, repairing a leaking roof, fixing cement cracks and so forth. Repairs do not add value to your home, only maintain it.

On the sale of your home, income tax rules require that you provide sufficient documentation to verify the tax basis of your home. This is used to determine your gain, which may qualify for an exclusion. Again, consult your tax advisor. Consequently, you should record and permanently retain any documents that relate to the tax basis of your home, including all home improvements. Add any notes of importance to the documents, such as dates, types of work done, and so forth.

To summarize your expenses and simplify the review of your documents, a tax work sheet is provided on the following page. The work sheet is easy to use for keeping an ongoing record of expenses for tax purposes. From your documents, transcribe all dates and costs associated with improvements such as renovation, remodeling, landscaping and other improvements that you make.

TAX WORK SHEET

Amount

Purchase Price of Home: _200,000_ _(10-2004)_

Additions to Basis: _____

Deed Taxes and Filing Fees: _____

Appraisal Fees: _____

Commissions to Brokers: _-0-_____

Legal Fees: _____

Escrow Fees: _____

Title Costs: _____

Other: _____

Major Renovation and Remodeling: _____

Date: _____

Major Renovation and Remodeling: _____

Date: _____

IMPORTANT PERSONAL PAPERS

List all your important personal papers and where you keep them. Your Will, life insurance policies, fire insurance policies, stocks and bonds are examples you need to list. Also list the location of your safe deposit box and all bank accounts. Include policy limits and the name of your attorney, agents, and brokers, etc. Tell your next of kin or other contact person(s) about this book and where you keep it.

Item   *Details*

_____

_____

_____

_____

_____

PURCHASE, FINANCE, & INSURANCE

PURCHASE INFORMATION

Date We Signed Purchase Contract: _____

Date We Closed Escrow: _____

Date We Moved In: _____

Date We Burnt Mortgage: _____

Date We Sold House: _____

Real Estate Company: _____

Agent: _____

Work Phone No.: _____

Home Phone No.: _____

BUILDING INFORMATION

Legal Address: (block, lot no., etc.): _6 Lorric Ln Lot 19_

Builder/Contractor's Company('s): _Wohlers Development Corp._

Contact Person(s): _David Wohlen_

Phone No.: _721- 1743_

Date Home Built (completed): _10 - 2004_

Warranty on Construction: _____

Land Development Company: _____

Phone No.: _____

Notes:

Photographs of House and Grounds:

FINANCE INFORMATION

Mortgage Company: _Charter One Mortgage_____

Loan Officer: _____

Work Phone No.: _____

Home Phone No.: _____

Loan No.: _____

Loan Servicing Dept. Phone No.: _____

New Mortgage Company (if your mortgage is sold): _____

Phone No.: _____

Date Sold: _____

Mortgage Balance at Time of Sale: _____

Notes:

Second Mortgage Company: _____

Phone No.: _____

Loan No.: _____

Date: _____

Balance of Principal on Original: _____

Mortgage Information: _____

Purchase Price: _____ Price Asked: _____

Down payment: _____ Appraised Value: _____

Mortgage Amount: _____

Location of Abstract: _____

Mortgage Type (FHA, VA, Conventional, etc.): _____

Interest Rate (beginning, if adjustable*): _____

Terms (30 yr. fixed, adjustable*, etc.):_____

Points (no. & amount): _____

Realtor's Commission (% & amt.): _____

Other Closing Costs:_____

Closing Date:_____

ADJUSTABLE RATE MORTGAGE (ARM):

Rate	Date of Change	Balance Remaining	Monthly P & I

Adjustment Interval:_____

Index: _____

Margin: _____

Interest Rate Caps (yearly, lifetime, etc.): _____

Monthly Payment Cap: _____

Graduated Payments:_____

Negative Amortization (y/n & limit):_____

Introductory Rate: _____

Assumability: _____

Convertibility:_____

Prepayment Privilege: _____

Points (including origination fee):_____

INSURANCE INFORMATION

Title Insurance Company: _____

Title Binder No.: _____

Homeowner's Insurance Company: _____

Agent's Name: _____

Work Phone No.: _____

Home Phone No.: _____

Policy No.: _____

Expiration Date (if prepaid): _____

EXTRA NOTES:

WARRANTIES

List here all items covered by a warranty

Item	Purchase Date	Expiration Date
YOUR HOME		
AIR CONDITIONER		
HOT WATER HEATER		
CARPET / VINYL		
DRIER		
DISH WASHER		
FOOD MIXER		
KITCHEN EQUIP.		
GARDEN EQUIP.		
SEPTIC SYSTEM		
T.V.		
VIDEO		
WASHING MACHINE		
WHIRLPOOL		
WINDOWS		
OTHERS		

BUILDING / REMODELING TIPS

HOW TO CHOOSE A BUILDER / CONTRACTOR

A.
- Ask your banker to refer names (They deal with builders all the time)
- Ask a lumber yard owner.
- Referrals from friends, relatives and acquaintances.
- Ask your Realtor.

B.
If you wish to do some of the work yourself, be sure to find a contractor willing to work with you as this can cause awkward situations for both of you.

C.
Make notes of all wallpaper, flooring, paint, tile etc. Without run #'s there is no guarantee of a match.

D.
Save extra a little of the paint or wallpaper for future repairs or additions

DOING IT YOURSELF

For those who are handy, experienced or brave of heart here are some do's and don'ts that can help you make it a fun experience.

Do
1. Go to seminars.
Your local Do It Yourself store may hold them.
2. Ask questions until you get a full answer
3. Do your homework and it will go easier.
4. Buy, rent or borrow the right tools for the job.
5. Hire a professional for any items that overwhelm you.

Don't
1. Start without a plan.
2. Rely on a friend/etc. whose work may pull him/her away.
3. Start without the correct tools.

GUTTERS & DOWN SPOUTS

Type of Material (plastic, metal, etc.): _Aluminum_

Supplied By: _____

Date: _____

Cost amt.: Warranty Period: _____

Installed By: _____

Date: _____

Notes:

ROOF

Type of Roof (tile, shingle, etc.): _____

Weatherproofing: _____

Supplied By: _____

Brand, Color, & No.: _____

Unit Cost: _____ No. of Units: _____

Extras: _____

Cost: _____

Total: _____

Contractor: _____

EXTERIOR (CONTINUED)

Cost:_____

Date: _____

Warranty Period:_____

Total Job Cost: _____

SIDING

1st. Type of Siding (brick, stucco, etc.): _____

Supplied By:_____

Date: _____ Cost:_____

Brand, Color, & No.: _____

Warranty Period:_____

Contractor:_____

Cost:_____ Date: _____

Type of Finish (paint, stain, etc.): _____

Supplied By:_____ Date: _____

Brand, Color, & No.: _____

Warranty Period:_____

Unit Cost: _____ No. of Units:_____ Total: _____

Contractor:_____

Date: _____ Cost:_____

Notes:

2nd. Type of Siding (brick, stucco, etc.): _____

Supplied By:_____

Date: _____ Cost:_____

Brand, Color, & No.: _____

Warranty Period: _____

Contractor: _____

Date: _____ Cost: _____

Type of Finish (paint, stain, etc.): _____

Supplied By: _____ Date: _____

Brand, Color, & No.: _____

Warranty Period: _____

Unit Cost: _____ No. of Units: _____ Total: _____

Contractor: _____

Date: _____ Cost: _____

Notes:

TRIM

1st. Type of Trim (wood, aluminum, etc.): _____

Supplied By: _____

Date: _____ Cost: _____

Brand, Color, & No.: _____

Warranty Period: _____

Contractor: _____

Type of Finish (paint, stain, etc.): _____

Supplied By: _____

Brand, Color, & No.: _____ Date: _____

Warranty Period: _____

Unit Cost: _____ No. of Units: _____ Total: _____

Contractor: _____

Date _____ Cost _____

EXTERIOR (CONTINUED)

2nd. Type of Trim (wood, aluminum, etc.) _____

Supplied By: _____

Date: _____ Cost: _____

Brand, Color, & No.: _____

Warranty Period: _____

Contractor: _____

Date: _____ Cost: _____

Type of Finish (paint, stain, etc.): _____

Supplied By: _____

Date: _____

Brand, Color, & No.: _____

Warranty Period: _____

Unit Cost: _____ No. of Units: _____ Total: _____

Contractor: _____

Date: _____ Cost: _____

Notes:

STORM DOORS

Supplied By: _____

Date: _____

Brand, Color, & No.: _____

Warranty Period: _____

Unit Cost: _____ No. of Units: _____ Total: _____

Contractor: _____

Date: _____ Cost: _____

STORM WINDOWS

Supplied By: _____

Date: _____

Brand, Color, & No.: _____

Warranty Period: _____

Unit Cost: _____ No. of Units: _____ Total: _____

Contractor: _____

Date: _____ Cost: _____

LANDSCAPE GARDENING
FRONT YARD

Contractor: _Scott + Bridget_____

Date(s): _5-30-05_____ Cost: _about $300___

Work Performed: _Built Medina Sandstone walls_____

Plantings: _Perennials / Weeping cherry / some annuals__

_____

_____

Masonry and Brick: _____

Contractor: _____

Date(s): _____ Cost: _____

Work Performed: _____

Plantings: _____

_____

_____

Masonry and Brick: _____

EXTERIOR (continued)

Side Yard

Contractor: _____

Date(s): _____ Cost: _____

Work Performed: _____

Plantings: _____

_____

_____

Masonry and Brick: _____

Contractor: _____

Date(s): _____ Cost: _____

Work Performed: _____

Plantings: _____

_____

_____

Masonry and Brick: _____

BACK YARD

Contractor: _____

Date(s): _____ Cost: _____

Work Performed: _____

Plantings: _____

_____

_____

Masonry and Brick: _____

Contractor: _____

Date(s): _____ Cost: _____

Work Performed: _____

Plantings: _____

_____

_____

Masonry and Brick: _____

POND

Contractor: _____

Date(s): _____ Cost: _____

Work Performed: _____

Plantings: _____

_____

_____

Masonry and Brick: _____

Contractor: _____

Date(s): _____ Cost: _____

Work Performed: _____

EXTERIOR (CONTINUED)

Repairs: _____

_____

_____

Notes:

GREENHOUSE

Contractor: _____

Date(s): _____ Cost: _____

Work Performed: _____

Plantings: _____

_____

_____

_____

_____

_____

Glazing & Repairs: _____

Contractor: _____

Date(s): _____ Cost: _____

Work Performed: _____

Plumbing: _____

Contractor: _____

Date(s): _____ Cost: _____

Work Performed: _____

Window Boxes

Contractor: _____

Date(s): _____ Cost: _____

Number and Locations: _____

Plantings: _____

Container Shrubs

Contractor: _____

Date(s): _____ Cost: _____

Number and Locations: _____

Plantings: _____

Contractor: _____

Date(s): _____ Cost: _____

Number and Locations: _____

Plantings: _____

Gazebo

Contractor: _____

Date(s): _____ Cost: _____

Type of Finish (paint, stain, etc.): _____

Supplied by: _____

Brand, Color, & No.: _____

Warranty Period: _____

Notes:

LIVING ROOM

FLOOR COVERING

Floor Size:

Measure from center of door to center of door, if any.

Width: _____ Length: _____ Total Sq. Ft/M.: _____

Type of Floor: (carpet, hardwood, etc.): _____

Supplied By: _____

Date: _____ Brand & Pattern: _____

Color & No.: _____

Unit Cost: _____ No. of Units: _____ Total: _____

Installed By: _____

Total: _____

Date: _____ Cost: _____

Serviced By: _____

Date 1: _____ Cost: _____

Date 2: _____ Cost: _____

Notes:

2ND FLOOR COVERING

2nd Floor Size:

Measure from center of door to center of door, if any.

Width: _____ Length: _____ Total Sq. Ft/M.: _____

Type of Floor: (carpet, hardwood, etc.): _____

Supplied By:_____

Date: _____ Brand & Pattern:_____

Color & No.:_____

Unit Cost: _____ No. of Units:_____ Total: _____

Installed By:_____

Total: _____

Date: _____ Cost:_____

Serviced By:_____

Date 1: _____ Cost:_____

Date 2: _____ Cost:_____

Notes:

CEILING FINISH

Type of Finish (paint, spray texture, etc.): _____

Supplied By:_____

Date: _____ Brand & Pattern:_____

Color & No.:_____

Unit Cost: _____ No. of Units _____ Total: _____

Installed By:_____

Date: _____ Cost:_____

Notes:

LIVING ROOM (CONTINUED)
CURTAINS, BLINDS, DRAPERIES

Window 1 Size:

Measure glass area inside window to be covered.

Height: _____ Width: _____ Total Sq. Ft./M.: _____

Floor to Sill Height: _____ Floor to Top of Window:_____

Multiple Window Width: _____ Height: _____

Type of Covering (draperies, blinds, etc.): _____

Supplied By: _____

Cost: _____ Date: _____

Measurements of Curtains, Blinds,Draperies: _____

Fabric & Cleaning Instructions: _____

Cleaned By: _____

Cost: _____ Date: _____

Notes:

Window 2 Size:

Measure glass area inside window to be covered.

Height: _____ Width: _____ Total Sq. Ft./M.: _____

Floor to Sill Height: _____ Floor to Top of Window:_____

Multiple Window Width: _____ Height: _____

Type of Covering (draperies, blinds, etc.): _____

Supplied By: _____

Cost: _____ Date: _____

Measurements of Curtains, Blinds, Draperies: _____

Fabric & Cleaning Instructions: _____

Cleaned By: _____

Cost:_____ Date: _____

Notes:

Window 3 Size:

Measure glass area inside window to be covered.

Height: _____ Width: _____ Total Sq. Ft./M.: _____

Floor to Sill Height: _____ Floor to Top of Window:_____

Multiple Window Width: _____ Height: _____

Type of Covering (draperies, blinds, etc.): _____

Supplied By:_____

Cost:_____ Date: _____

Measurements of Curtains, Blinds, Draperies: _____

Fabric & Cleaning Instructions: _____

Cleaned By: _____

Cost:_____ Date: _____

Notes:

Window 4 Size:

Measure glass area inside window to be covered.

Height: _____ Width: _____ Total Sq. Ft./M.: _____

Floor to Sill Height: _____ Floor to Top of Window:_____

Multiple Window Width: _____ Height: _____

Type of Covering (draperies, blinds, etc.): _____

LIVING ROOM (CONTINUED)

Supplied By:_____

Cost:_____ Date: _____

Measurements of Curtains, Blinds, Draperies: _____

Fabric & Cleaning Instructions: _____

Cleaned By: _____

Cost:_____ Date: _____

Notes:

WALL FINISH

Wall Sizes:

North: _____ South: _____ East: _____ West: _____

Total Sq. Ft./M.: _____

1st. Type of Finish (paint, paper, etc.): _____

Supplied By:_____

Date: _____ Brand & Pattern:_____

Color & No: _____

Unit Cost: _____ No. of Units:_____ Total: _____

Installed By:_____

Date: _____ Cost:_____

2nd. Type of Finish (woodwork, paneling, etc.): _____

Supplied By:_____

Date: _____ Brand & Pattern:_____

Color & No.:_____

Unit Cost: _____ No. of Units:_____ Total: _____

Installed By:_____

Date: _____ Cost:_____

Refinished By:_____

Date: _____ Cost:_____

Notes:

SAMPLES: PAINT, WALLPAPER, ETC.

attach wallpaper sample or daub paint sample here

CEILING FANS

Manufacturer & Model:_____

Supplied By:_____

Date: _____ Cost:_____

Warranty Period:_____

Installed By:_____

Date: _____ Cost:_____

Notes:

Manufacturer & Model:_____

Supplied By:_____

Date: _____ Cost:_____

Warranty Period:_____

Installed By:_____

Date: _____ Cost:_____

Notes:

PARLOR

FLOOR COVERING

Floor Size:

Measure from center of door to center of door, if any.

Width: _____ Length: _____ Total Sq. Ft./M.: _____

Type of Floor: (carpet, hardwood, etc.): _____

Supplied By: _____

Date: _____ Brand & Pattern: _____

Color & No.: _____

Unit Cost: _____ No. of Units: _____ Total: _____

Installed By: _____

Total: _____

Date: _____ Cost: _____

Serviced By: _____ Date 1: _____ Cost: _____

Serviced By: _____ Date 2: _____ Cost: _____

Notes:

CEILING FINISH

Type of Finish (paint, spray texture, etc.): _____

Supplied By: _____

Date: _____ Brand & Pattern: _____

Color & No.: _____

Unit Cost: _____ No. of Units _____ Total: _____

Installed By: _____

Date: _____ Cost: _____

CURTAINS BLINDS, DRAPERIES

Window 1 Size:

Measure glass area inside window to be covered.

Height: _____ Width: _____ Total Sq. Ft./M.: _____

Floor to Sill Height: _____ Floor to Top of Window: _____

Multiple Window Width: _____ Height: _____

Type of Covering (draperies, blinds, etc.): _____

Supplied By: _____

Cost: _____ Date: _____

Measurements of Curtains, Blinds, Draperies: _____

Fabric & Cleaning Instructions: _____

Cleaned By: _____

Cost: _____ Date: _____

PARLOR (continued)

Window 2 Size:

Measure glass area inside window to be covered.

Height: _____ Width: _____ Total Sq. Ft./M.: _____

Floor to Sill Height: _____ Floor to Top of Window: _____

Multiple Window Width: _____ Height: _____

Type of Covering (draperies, blinds, etc.): _____

Supplied By: _____

Cost: _____ Date: _____

Measurements of Curtains, Blinds, Draperies: _____

Fabric & Cleaning Instructions: _____

Cleaned By: _____

Cost: _____ Date: _____

Window 3 Size:

Measure glass area inside window to be covered.

Height: _____ Width: _____ Total Sq. Ft./M.: _____

Floor to Sill Height: _____ Floor to Top of Window: _____

Multiple Window Width: _____ Height: _____

Type of Covering (draperies, blinds, etc.): _____

Supplied By: _____

Cost: _____ Date: _____

Measurements of Curtains, Blinds, Draperies: _____

Fabric & Cleaning Instructions: _____

Cleaned By: _____

Cost: _____ Date: _____

Notes:

WALL FINISH

Wall Sizes:

North: _____ South: _____ East: _____ West: _____

Total Sq. Ft./M.: _____

1st Type of Finish (paint, paper, etc.): _____

Supplied By: _____

Date: _____ Brand & Pattern: _____

Color & No: _____

Unit Cost: _____ No. of Units: _____ Total: _____

Installed By: _____

Date: _____ Cost: _____

Notes:

2nd. Type of Finish (woodwork, paneling, etc.) _____

Supplied By: _____

Date: _____ Brand & Pattern: _____

Color & No.: _____

Unit Cost: _____ No. of Units: _____ Total: _____

Installed By: _____

Date: _____ Cost: _____

Refinished By: _____

Date: _____ Cost: _____

Notes:

SAMPLES: PAINT, WALLPAPER, ETC.

attach wallpaper sample or daub paint sample here

FURNITURE / APPLIANCES

Item	Supplied By	Date	Cost	Warranty

KITCHEN

FLOOR COVERING

Floor Size:

Measure from center of door to center of door, if any.

Width: _____ Length: _____ Total Sq. Ft./M.: _____

Type of Floor (carpet, tile, etc.): _____

Supplied By: _____ Date: _____

Brand & Pattern: _____

Color & No.: _____

Unit Cost: _____ No. of Units: _____ Total: _____

Installed By: _____

Date: _____ Cost: _____

Serviced By: _____

Date 1: _____ Cost: _____

Date 2: _____ Cost: _____

Notes:

CEILING FINISH

Type of Finish (paint, spray texture, etc.): _____

Supplied By: _____

Date: _____ Brand & Pattern: _____

Color & No: _____

Unit Cost: _____ No. of Units: _____ Total: _____

Installed By: _____

Date: _____ Cost: _____

CURTAINS, BLINDS, DRAPERIES

Window 1 Sizes:

Measure glass area inside window to be covered.

Height: _____ Width: _____ Total Sq. Ft./M.: _____

Floor to Sill Height: _____ Floor to Top of Window:_____

Multiple Window Width: _____ Height: _____

Type of Covering (draperies, blinds, etc.): _____

Supplied By:_____

Cost:_____ Date: _____

Measurements of Curtains, Blinds, Draperies: _____

Fabric & Cleaning Instructions: _____

Cleaned By: _____

Cost:_____ Date: _____

Window 2 Sizes:

Measure glass area inside window to be covered.

Height: _____ Width: _____ Total Sq. Ft./M.: _____

Floor to Sill Height: _____ Floor to Top of Window:_____

Multiple Window Width: _____ Height: _____

Type of Covering (draperies, blinds, etc.):_____

Supplied By:_____

Cost:_____ Date: _____

Measurements of Curtains, Blinds, Draperies: _____

Fabric & Cleaning Instructions: _____

Cleaned By: _____

Cost:_____ Date: _____

WALL FINISH

Wall Sizes: _____

North: _____ South: _____ East: _____ West: _____

Total Sq. Ft./M.: _____

1st. Type of Finish (paint, paper, etc.): _____

Supplied By:_____

Date: _____ Brand & Pattern:_____

Unit Cost: _____ No. of Units:_____ Total: _____

Installed By:_____

Date: _____ Cost:_____

Notes:

2nd. Type of Finish (woodwork, paneling, etc.): _____

Supplied By:_____

Date: _____ Brand & Pattern:_____

Color & No.:_____

Unit Cost: _____ No. of Units:_____ Total: _____

Installed By:_____

Date: _____ Cost:_____

Refinished By:_____

Date: _____ Cost:_____

Notes:

CABINETS

Supplied By:_____ Date: _____

Brand & Style: _____

Cost:_____ Stain Color & No.: _____

KITCHEN (CONTINUED)

Warranty: _____

Type of Wood (oak, pine, etc.): _____

Finished With (polyurethane, varnish, etc.): _____

Countertop Material (laminate, etc.): _____

Brand & Pattern: _____ Color & No.: _____

Installed By: _____

Date: _____ Cost: _____

Refinished By: _____

Refinished With: _____

Date: _____ Cost: _____

Notes:

FURNITURE / APPLIANCES

Item	Supplied By	Date	Cost	Warranty

SAMPLES: PAINT, WALLPAPER, ETC.

attach wallpaper sample or daub paint sample here

MAJOR APPLIANCES

Type of Appliance (range, dishwasher, etc.): _____

Supplied By: _Page Appliances_ _____

Manufacturer: _____

Date: _____ Cost: _____

Model/Lot/Serial No.: _____

Authorized Service Center: _____

Warranty Period: _____

Notes:

Type of Appliance (range, dishwasher, etc.): _____

Supplied By: _____

Manufacturer: _____

Date: _____ Cost: _____

Model/Lot/Serial No.: _____

Authorized Service Center: _____

Warranty Period: _____

Notes:

Type of Appliance (range, dishwasher, etc.): _____

Supplied By: _____

Manufacturer: _____

KITCHEN (CONTINUED)

Date: _____ Cost: _____

Model/Lot/Serial No.: _____

Authorized Service Center: _____

Warranty Period: _____

Notes:

BREAKFAST NOOK

Type of Wood (oak, pine, etc.): _____

Finished With (polyurethane, varnish, etc.): _____

Countertop Material (laminate, etc.): _____

Brand & Pattern: _____ Color & No.: _____

Installed By: _____

Date: _____ Cost: _____

Refinished By: _____

Refinished With: _____

Date: _____ Cost: _____

Notes:

DINING ROOM

FLOOR COVERING

Floor Size:

Measure from center of door to center of door, if any.

Width: _____ Length: _____ Total Sq. Ft./M.: _____

Type of Floor: (carpet, hardwood, etc.): _____

Supplied By: _____

Date: _____ Brand & Pattern: _____

Color & No.: _____

Unit Cost: _____ No. of Units: _____ Total: _____

Installed By: _____

Total: _____

Date: _____ Cost: _____

Serviced By: _____

Date 1: _____ Cost: _____

Date 2: _____ Cost: _____

Notes:

CEILING FINISH

Type of Finish (paint, spray texture, etc.): _____

Supplied By: _____

Date: _____ Brand & Pattern: _____

Color & No: _____

Unit Cost: _____ No. of Units: _____ Total: _____

DINING ROOM (continued)

Installed By:_____

Date: _____ Cost:_____

Notes:

CEILING FAN

Manufacturer & Model:_____

Supplied By:_____

Date: _____ Cost:_____

Warranty Period:_____

Installed By:_____

Date: _____ Cost:_____

Notes:

CURTAINS, BLINDS, DRAPERIES

Window 1 Size:

Measure glass area inside window to be covered.

Height: _____ Width: _____ Total Sq. Ft./M.: _____

Floor to Sill Height: _____ Floor to Top of Window:_____

Multiple Window Width: _____ Height: _____

Type of Covering (draperies, blinds, etc.):_____

Supplied By:_____

Cost:_____ Date: _____

Measurements of Curtains, Blinds, Draperies: _____

Fabric & Cleaning Instructions: _____

Cleaned By: _____

Cost:_____ Date: _____

WALL FINISH

Wall Sizes:

North: _____ South: _____ East: _____ West: _____

Total Sq. Ft./M.: _____

1st. Type of Finish (paint, paper, etc.): _____

Supplied By: _____

Date: _____ Brand & Pattern: _____

Color & No: _____

Unit Cost: _____ No. of Units: _____ Total: _____

Installed By: _____

Date: _____ Cost: _____

Notes:

2nd. Type of Finish (woodwork, paneling, etc.): _____

Supplied By: _____

Date: _____ Brand & Pattern: _____

Color & No.: _____

Unit Cost: _____ No. of Units: _____ Total: _____

Installed By: _____

Date: _____ Cost: _____

Refinished By: _____

Date: _____ Cost: _____

Notes:

SAMPLES: PAINT, WALLPAPER, ETC.

attach wallpaper sample or daub paint sample here

FURNITURE / APPLIANCES

Item	Supplied By	Date	Cost	Warranty

LIBRARY / STUDY / DEN

FLOOR COVERING

Floor Size:

Measure from center of door to center of door, if any.

Width: _____ Length: _____ Total Sq. Ft./M.: _____

Type of Floor: (carpet, hardwood, etc.): _____

Supplied By: _____

Date: _____ Brand & Pattern: _____

Color & No.: _____

Unit Cost: _____ No. of Units: _____ Total: _____

Installed By: _____

Total: _____

Date: _____ Cost: _____

Serviced By: _____

Date 1: _____ Cost:_____

Date 2: _____ Cost:_____

Notes:

CEILING FINISH

Type of Finish (paint, spray texture, etc.): _____

Supplied By:_____

Date: _____ Brand & Pattern:_____

Color & No.:_____

Unit Cost: _____ No. of Units _____ Total: _____

Installed By:_____

Date: _____ Cost:_____

Notes:

CEILING FAN

Manufacturer & Model:_____

Supplied By:_____

Date: _____ Cost:_____

Warranty Period:_____

Installed By:_____

Date: _____ Cost:_____

Notes:

CURTAINS, BLINDS, DRAPERIES

Window 1 Size:

Measure glass area inside window to be covered.

LIBRARY / STUDY / DEN (CONTINUED)

Height: _____ Width: _____ Total Sq. Ft./M.: _____

Floor to Sill Height: _____ Floor to Top of Window: _____

Multiple Window Width: _____ Height: _____

Type of Covering (draperies, blinds, etc.): _____

Supplied By: _____

Cost: _____ Date: _____

Measurements of Curtains, Blinds, Draperies: _____

Fabric & Cleaning Instructions: _____

Cleaned By: _____

Cost: _____ Date: _____

Notes:

Window 2 Size:

Measure glass area inside window to be covered.

Height: _____ Width: _____ Total Sq. Ft./M.: _____

Floor to Sill Height: _____ Floor to Top of Window: _____

Multiple Window Width: _____ Height: _____

Type of Covering (draperies, blinds, etc.): _____

Supplied By: _____

Cost: _____ Date: _____

Measurements of Curtains, Blinds, Draperies: _____

Fabric & Cleaning Instructions: _____

Cleaned By: _____

Cost: _____ Date: _____

Notes:

WALL FINISH

Wall Sizes:

North: _____ South: _____ East: _____ West: _____

Total Sq. Ft./M.: _____

1st. Type of Finish (paint, paper, etc.): _____

Supplied By: _____

Date: _____ Brand & Pattern: _____

Color & No: _____

Unit Cost: _____ No. of Units: _____ Total: _____

Installed By: _____

Date: _____ Cost: _____

2nd. Type of Finish (woodwork, paneling, etc.): _____

Supplied By: _____

Date: _____ Brand & Pattern: _____

Color & No.: _____

Unit Cost: _____ No. of Units: _____ Total: _____

Installed By: _____

Date: _____ Cost: _____

Refinished By: _____

Date: _____ Cost: _____

Notes:

SAMPLES: PAINT, WALLPAPER, ETC.

attach wallpaper sample or daub paint sample here

WALL SHELVES

Type of Finish (paint, varnish, etc.): _____

Supplied By: _____

Date: _____ Brand & Pattern: _____

Color & No.: _____

Unit Cost: _____ No. of Units _____ Total: _____

Installed By: _____

Date: _____ Cost: _____

Notes:

FURNITURE / APPLIANCES

Item	Supplied By	Date	Cost	Warranty

FAMILY ROOM

FLOOR COVERING

Floor Size:

Measure from center of door to center of door, if any.

Width: _____ Length: _____ Total Sq. Ft./M.: _____

Type of Floor: (carpet, hardwood, etc.): _____

Supplied By:_____

Date: _____ Brand & Pattern:_____

Color & No.:_____

Unit Cost: _____ No. of Units:_____ Total: _____

Installed By:_____

Total: _____

Date: _____ Cost:_____

Serviced By:_____

Date 1: _____ Cost:_____

Date 2: _____ Cost:_____

Notes:

CEILING FINISH

Type of Finish (paint, spray texture, etc.): _____

Supplied By:_____

Date: _____ Brand & Pattern:_____

Color & No.:_____

Unit Cost: _____ No. of Units _____ Total: _____

Installed By:_____

Date: _____ Cost:_____

CURTAINS, BLINDS, DRAPERIES

Window 1 Size:

Measure glass area inside window to be covered.

Height: _____ Width: _____ Total Sq. Ft./M.: _____

Floor to Sill Height: _____ Floor to Top of Window:_____

Multiple Window Width: _____ Height: _____

Type of Covering (draperies, blinds, etc.):_____

Supplied By:_____

Cost:_____ Date: _____

Measurements of Curtains, Blinds, Draperies: _____

Fabric & Cleaning Instructions: _____

Cleaned By: _____

Cost:_____ Date: _____

Notes:

Window 2 Size:

Measure glass area inside window to be covered.

Height: _____ Width: _____ Total Sq. Ft./M.: _____

Floor to Sill Height: _____ Floor to Top of Window:_____

Multiple Window Width: _____ Height: _____

Type of Covering (draperies, blinds, etc.):_____

Supplied By:_____

Cost:_____ Date: _____

Measurements of Curtains, Blinds, Draperies: _____

Fabric & Cleaning Instructions: _____

Cleaned By: _____

FAMILY ROOM (continued)

Cost:_____ Date: _____

Notes:

CEILING FAN

Manufacturer & Model:_____

Supplied By:_____

Date: _____ Cost:_____

Warranty Period:_____

Installed By:_____

Date: _____ Cost:_____

Notes:

WALL FINISH

Wall Sizes:

North: _____ South: _____ East: _____ West _____

Total Sq. Ft./M.: _____

1st. Type of Finish (paint, paper, etc.): _____

Supplied By:_____

Date: _____ Brand & Pattern:_____

Color & No: _____

Unit Cost: _____ No. of Units:_____ Total: _____

Installed By:_____

Date: _____ Cost:_____

Notes:

2nd. Type of Finish (woodwork, paneling, etc.): _____

Supplied By: _____

Date: _____ Brand & Pattern: _____

Color & No.: _____

Unit Cost: _____ No. of Units: _____ Total: _____

Installed By: _____

Date: _____ Cost: _____

Refinished By: _____

Date: _____ Cost: _____

Notes:

SAMPLES: PAINT, WALLPAPER, ETC.

attach wallpaper sample or daub paint sample here

FURNITURE / APPLIANCES

Item	Supplied By	Date	Cost	Warranty

FAMILY ROOM (CONTINUED)

HOME ENTERTAINMENT CENTER

Television: _____

Model/Lot/Serial No.: _____

Supplied By: _____

Date: _____ Cost: _____

Authorized Service Center: _____

Warranty Period: _____

Video Cassette Recorder: _____

Model/Lot/Serial No.: _____

Supplied By: _____

Date: _____ Cost: _____

Authorized Service Center: _____

Warranty Period: _____

Stereo and Entertainment Components:

Item	Supplied By	Date	Cost	Warranty

Cabinets Supplied By: _____

Date: _____ Cost: _____

ENTRY / MUD ROOM

FLOOR COVERING

Floor Size:

Width: _____ Length: _____ Total Sq. Ft./M.: _____

Type of Floor (carpet, tile, etc.): _____

Supplied By: _____

Date: _____

Brand & Pattern: _____

Color & No.: _____

Unit Cost: _____ No. of Units: _____ Total: _____

Installed By: _____

Date: _____ Cost: _____

Serviced By: _____

Date 1: _____ Cost: _____

Date 2: _____ Cost: _____

Notes:

CEILING FINISH

Type of Finish (paint, spray texture, etc.): _____

Supplied By: _____

Date: _____

Brand & Pattern: _____ Color & No.: _____

Unit Cost: _____ No. of Units: _____ Total: _____

Installed By: _____

Date: _____ Cost: _____

CURTAINS, BLINDS, DRAPERIES

Window Size:

Measure glass area inside window to be covered.

Height: _____ Width: _____ Total Sq. Ft./M.: _____

Floor to Sill Height: _____ Floor to Top of Window: _____

Multiple Window Width:Height: _____

Type of Covering (draperies, blinds, etc.): _____

Supplied By: _____

Cost: _____ Date: _____

Measurements of Curtains, Blinds, Draperies: _____

Fabric & Cleaning Instructions: _____

Cleaned By: _____

Cost: _____ Date: _____

Notes:

WALL FINISH

Wall Size:

Measure from center of door to center of door, if any.

North: _____ South: _____ East: _____ West: _____

Total Sq. Ft./M.: _____

1st. Type of Covering (paint, paper, etc.): _____

Supplied By: _____

Date: _____

Brand & Pattern: _____ Color & No.: _____

Unit Cost: _____ No. of Units:_____ Total: _____

Installed By:_____

Date: _____ Cost:_____

Notes:

2nd. Type of Covering (woodwork, paneling, etc.):

Supplied By:_____

Date: _____ Brand pattern: _____

Color & No.:_____

Unit Cost: _____ No. of Units:_____ Total: _____

Installed By:_____

Date: _____ Cost:_____

Refinished By:_____

Date: _____ Cost:_____

SAMPLES: PAINT, WALLPAPER, ETC.

attach wallpaper sample or daub paint sample here

FLOOR COVERING

Floor Size:

Measure from center of door to center of door, if any.

Width: _____ Length: _____ Total Sq. Ft./M.: _____

Type of Floor: (carpet, hardwood, etc.): _____

Supplied By: _____

Date: _____ Brand & Pattern: _____

Color & No.: _____

Unit Cost: _____ No. of Units: _____ Total: _____

Installed By: _____

Total: _____

Date: _____ Cost: _____

Serviced By: _____

Date 1: _____ Cost: _____

Date 2: _____ Cost: _____

Notes:

CEILING FINISH

Type of Finish (paint, spray texture, etc.): _____

Supplied By: _____

Date: _____ Brand & Pattern: _____

Color & No.: _____

Unit Cost: _____ No. of Units _____ Total: _____

Installed By: _____

Date: _____ Cost: _____

Notes:

CURTAINS, BLINDS, DRAPERIES

Window 1 Size:

Measure glass area inside window to be covered.

Height: _____ Width: _____ Total Sq. Ft./M.: _____

Floor to Sill Height: _____ Floor to Top of Window: _____

Multiple Window Width: _____ Height: _____

Type of Covering (draperies, blinds, etc.): _____

Supplied By: _____

Cost: _____ Date: _____

Measurements of Curtains, Blinds, Draperies: _____

Fabric & Cleaning Instructions: _____

Cleaned By: _____

Cost: _____ Date: _____

Notes:

HALLWAY / STAIRWAY (CONTINUED)

Window 2 Size:

Measure glass area inside window to be covered.

Height: _____ Width: _____ Total Sq. Ft./M.: _____

Floor to Sill Height: _____ Floor to Top of Window:_____

Multiple Window Width: _____ Height: _____

Type of Covering (draperies, blinds, etc.):_____

Supplied By:_____

Cost:_____ Date: _____

Measurements of Curtains, Blinds, Draperies: _____

Fabric & Cleaning Instructions: _____

Cleaned By: _____

Cost:_____ Date: _____

Notes:

WALL FINISH

Wall Sizes:

North: _____ South: _____ East: _____ West: _____

Total Sq. Ft./M.: _____

1st. Type of Finish (paint, paper, etc.): _____

Supplied By:_____

Date: _____ Brand & Pattern:_____

Color & No: _____

Unit Cost: _____ No. of Units:_____ Total: _____

Installed By:_____

Date: _____ Cost:_____

Notes:

2nd. Type of Finish (woodwork, paneling, etc.): _____

Supplied By:_____

Date: _____ Brand & Pattern:_____

Color & No.:_____

Unit Cost: _____ No. of Units:_____ Total: _____

Installed By:_____

Date: _____ Cost:_____

Refinished By:_____

Date: _____ Cost:_____

Notes:

SAMPLES: PAINT, WALLPAPER, ETC.

attach wallpaper sample or daub paint sample here

FLOOR COVERING

Floor Size:

Measure from center of door to center of door, if any.

Width: _____ Length: _____ Total Sq. Ft./M.: _____

Type of Floor: (carpet, hardwood, etc.): _____

Supplied By: _____

Date: _____ Brand & Pattern: _____

Color & No.: _____

Unit Cost: _____ No. of Units: _____ Total: _____

Installed By: _____

Total: _____

Date: _____ Cost: _____

Serviced By: _____

Date 1: _____ Cost: _____

Date 2: _____ Cost: _____

Notes:

CEILING FINISH

Type of Finish (paint, spray texture, etc.): _____

Supplied By: _____

Date: _____ Brand & Pattern: _____

Color & No.: _____

Unit Cost: _____ No. of Units _____ Total: _____

Installed By: _____

Date: _____ Cost: _____

CURTAINS, BLINDS, DRAPERIES

Window 1 Size:

Measure glass area inside window to be covered.

Height: _____ Width: _____ Total Sq. Ft./M.: _____

Floor to Sill Height: _____ Floor to Top of Window: _____

Multiple Window Width: _____ Height: _____

Type of Covering (draperies, blinds, etc.): _____

Supplied By: _____

Cost: _____ Date: _____

Measurements of Curtains, Blinds, Draperies: _____

Fabric & Cleaning Instructions: _____

Cleaned By: _____

Cost: _____ Date: _____

Window 2 Size:

Measure glass area inside window to be covered.

Height: _____ Width: _____ Total Sq. Ft./M.: _____

Floor to Sill Height: _____ Floor to Top of Window: _____

Multiple Window Width: _____ Height: _____

Type of Covering (draperies, blinds, etc.): _____

Supplied By: _____

Cost: _____ Date: _____

Measurements of Curtains, Blinds, Draperies: _____

Fabric & Cleaning Instructions: _____

Cleaned By: _____

Cost: _____ Date: _____

WALL FINISH

Wall Sizes:

North: _____ South: _____ East: _____ West: _____

Total Sq. Ft./M.: _____

1st. Type of Finish (paint, paper, etc.): _____

Supplied By: _____

Date: _____ Brand & Pattern: _____

Color & No: _____

Unit Cost: _____ No. of Units: _____ Total: _____

Installed By: _____

Date: _____ Cost: _____

2nd. Type of Finish (woodwork, paneling, etc.): _____

Supplied By: _____

Date: _____ Brand & Pattern: _____

Color & No.: _____

Unit Cost: _____ No. of Units: _____ Total: _____

Installed By: _____

Date: _____ Cost: _____

Refinished By: _____

Date: _____ Cost: _____

Notes:

SAMPLES: PAINT, WALLPAPER, ETC.

attach wallpaper sample or daub paint sample here

FURNITURE / APPLIANCES

Item	Supplied By	Date	Cost	Warranty

HALLWAY / STAIRWAY 3

FLOOR COVERING

Floor Size:

Measure from center of door to center of door, if any.

Width: _____ Length: _____ Total Sq. Ft./M.: _____

Type of Floor: (carpet, hardwood, etc.): _____

Supplied By: _____

Date: _____ Brand & Pattern: _____

Color & No.: _____

Unit Cost: _____ No. of Units: _____ Total: _____

Installed By: _____

Total: _____

Date: _____ Cost: _____

Serviced By: _____

Date 1: _____ Cost: _____

Date 2: _____ Cost: _____

Notes:

CEILING FINISH

Type of Finish (paint, spray texture, etc.): _____

Supplied By: _____

Date: _____ Brand & Pattern: _____

Color & No.: _____

Unit Cost: _____ No. of Units _____ Total: _____

Installed By: _____

Date: _____ Cost: _____

Notes:

CURTAINS, BLINDS, DRAPERIES

Window 1 Size:

Measure glass area inside window to be covered.

Height: _____ Width: _____ Total Sq. Ft./M.: _____

Floor to Sill Height: _____ Floor to Top of Window: _____

Multiple Window Width: _____ Height: _____

Type of Covering (draperies, blinds, etc.): _____

Supplied By: _____

Cost: _____ Date: _____

Measurements of Curtains, Blinds, Draperies: _____

Fabric & Cleaning Instructions: _____

Cleaned By: _____

Cost: _____ Date: _____

Notes:

Window 2 Size:

Measure glass area inside window to be covered.

Height: _____ Width: _____ Total Sq. Ft./M.: _____

Floor to Sill Height: _____ Floor to Top of Window:_____

Multiple Window Width: _____ Height: _____

Type of Covering (draperies, blinds, etc.): _____

Supplied By:_____

Cost:_____ Date: _____

Measurements of Curtains, Blinds, Draperies: _____

Fabric & Cleaning Instructions: _____

Cleaned By: _____

Cost:_____ Date: _____

Notes:

WALL FINISH

Wall Sizes:

North: _____ South: _____ East: _____ West: _____

Total Sq. Ft./M.: _____

1st. Type of Finish (paint, paper, etc.): _____

Supplied By:_____

Date: _____ Brand & Pattern:_____

Color & No: _____

Unit Cost: _____ No. of Units:_____ Total: _____

Installed By:_____

Date: _____ Cost:_____

Notes:

2nd. Type of Finish (woodwork, paneling, etc.): _____

Supplied By:_____

Date: _____ Brand & Pattern:_____

Color & No.:_____

Unit Cost: _____ No. of Units:_____ Total: _____

Installed By:_____

Date: _____ Cost:_____

Refinished By:_____

Date: _____ Cost:_____

Notes:

SAMPLES: PAINT, WALLPAPER, ETC.

attach wallpaper sample or daub paint sample here

FLOOR COVERING

Floor Size:

Measure from center of door to center of door, if any.

Width: _____ Length: _____ Total Sq. Ft./M.: _____

Type of Floor: (carpet, hardwood, etc.): _____

Supplied By: _____

Date: _____ Brand & Pattern: _____

Color & No.: _____

Unit Cost: _____ No. of Units: _____ Total: _____

Installed By: _____

Total: _____

Date: _____ Cost: _____

Serviced By: _____

Date 1: _____ Cost: _____

Date 2: _____ Cost: _____

Notes:

CEILING FINISH

Type of Finish (paint, spray texture, etc.): _____

Supplied By: _____

Date: _____ Brand & Pattern: _____

Color & No.: _____

Unit Cost: _____ No. of Units _____ Total: _____

Date: _____ Cost: _____

Notes:

CURTAINS, BLINDS, DRAPERIES

Window Size:

Measure glass area inside window to be covered.

Height: _____ Width: _____ Total Sq. Ft./M.: _____

Floor to Sill Height: _____ Floor to Top of Window: _____

Multiple Window Width: _____ Height: _____

Type of Covering (draperies, blinds, etc.): _____

Supplied By: _____

Cost: _____ Date: _____

Measurements of Curtains, Blinds, Draperies: _____

Fabric & Cleaning Instructions: _____

Cleaned By: _____

Cost: _____ Date: _____

Notes:

WALL FINISH

Wall Sizes:

North: _____ South: _____ East: _____ West: _____

Total Sq. Ft./M.: _____

1st. Type of Finish (paint, paper, etc.): _____

Supplied By: _____

Date: _____ Brand & Pattern: _____

Color & No: _____

Unit Cost: _____ No. of Units:_____ Total: _____

Installed By:_____

Date: _____ Cost:_____

Notes:

2nd. Type of Finish (woodwork, paneling, etc.): _____

Supplied By:_____

Date: _____ Brand & Pattern:_____

Color & No.:_____

Unit Cost: _____ No. of Units:_____ Total: _____

Installed By:_____

Date: _____ Cost:_____

Refinished By:_____

Date: _____ Cost:_____

Notes:

SAMPLES: PAINT, WALLPAPER, ETC.

attach wallpaper sample or daub paint sample here

LAUNDRY ROOM (continued)

MAJOR APPLIANCES

Type of Appliance (washer, dryer, etc.): _____

Supplied By: _____

Manufacturer: _____

Date: _____ Cost: _____

Model/Lot/Serial No.: _____

Authorized Service Center: _____

Warranty Period: _____

Type of Appliance (washer, dryer, etc.): _____

Supplied By: _____

Manufacturer: _____

Date: _____ Cost: _____

Model/Lot/Serial No.: _____

Authorized Service Center: _____

Warranty Period: _____

Type of Appliance (washer, dryer, etc.): _____

Supplied By: _____

Manufacturer: _____

Date: _____ Cost: _____

Model/Lot/Serial No.: _____

Authorized Service Center: _____

Warranty Period: _____

BEDROOM NUMBER 1

FLOOR COVERING

Floor Size:

Measure from center of door to center of door, if any.

Width: _____ Length: _____ Total Sq. Ft./M.: _____

Type of Floor: (carpet, hardwood, etc.): _____

Supplied By: _____

Date: _____ Brand & Pattern: _____

Color & No.: _____

Unit Cost: _____ No. of Units: _____ Total: _____

Installed By: _____

Total: _____

Date: _____ Cost: _____

Serviced By: _____

Date 1: _____ Cost: _____

Date 2: _____ Cost: _____

Notes:

CEILING FINISH

Type of Finish (paint, spray texture, etc.): _____

Supplied By: _____

Date: _____ Brand & Pattern: _____

Color & No.: _____

Unit Cost: _____ No. of Units _____ Total: _____

Installed By: _____

BEDROOM (CONTINUED)

Date: _____ Cost:_____

Notes:

CURTAINS, BLINDS, DRAPERIES

Window 1 Size:

Measure glass area inside window to be covered.

Height: _____ Width: _____ Total Sq. Ft./M.: _____

Floor to Sill Height: _____ Floor to Top of Window:_____

Multiple Window Width: _____ Height: _____

Type of Covering (draperies, blinds, etc.):_____

Supplied By:_____

Cost:_____ Date: _____

Measurements of Curtains, Blinds, Draperies: _____

Fabric & Cleaning Instructions: _____

Cleaned By: _____

Cost:_____ Date: _____

Notes:

Window 2 Size:

Measure glass area inside window to be covered.

Height: _____ Width: _____ Total Sq. Ft./M.: _____

Floor to Sill Height: _____ Floor to Top of Window:_____

Multiple Window Width: _____ Height: _____

Type of Covering (draperies, blinds, etc.):_____

Supplied By:_____

Cost:_____ Date: _____

Measurements of Curtains, Blinds, Draperies: _____

Fabric & Cleaning Instructions: _____

Cleaned By: _____

Cost:_____ Date: _____

WALL FINISH

Wall Sizes:

North: _____ South: _____ East: _____ West: _____

Total Sq. Ft./M.: _____

1st. Type of Finish (paint, paper, etc.): _____

Supplied By:_____

Date: _____ Brand & Pattern:_____

Color & No: _____

Unit Cost: _____ No. of Units:_____ Total: _____

Installed By:_____

Date: _____ Cost:_____

2nd. Type of Finish (woodwork, paneling, etc.): _____

Supplied By:_____

Date: _____ Brand & Pattern:_____

Color & No.:_____

Unit Cost: _____ No. of Units:_____ Total: _____

Installed By:_____

Date: _____ Cost:_____

Refinished By:_____

Date: _____ Cost:_____

Notes:

SAMPLES: PAINT, WALLPAPER, ETC.

attach wallpaper sample or daub paint sample here

FURNITURE / APPLIANCES

Item	Supplied By	Date	Cost	Warranty

BEDROOM NUMBER 2

FLOOR COVERING

Floor Size:

Measure from center of door to center of door, if any.

Width: _____ Length: _____ Total Sq. Ft./M.: _____

Type of Floor: (carpet, hardwood, etc.): _____

Supplied By:_____

Date: _____ Brand & Pattern:_____

Color & No.:_____

Unit Cost: _____ No. of Units:_____ Total: _____

Installed By:_____

Total: _____

Date: _____ Cost:_____

Serviced By:_____

Date 1: _____ Cost:_____

Date 2: _____ Cost:_____

Notes:

CEILING FINISH

Type of Finish (paint, spray texture, etc.): _____

Supplied By:_____

Date: _____ Brand & Pattern:_____

Color & No.:_____

Unit Cost: _____ No. of Units _____ Total: _____

Installed By:_____

BEDROOM (CONTINUED)

Date: _____ Cost:_____

Notes:

CURTAINS, BLINDS, DRAPERIES

Window 1 Size:

Measure glass area inside window to be covered.

Height: _____ Width: _____ Total Sq. Ft./M.: _____

Floor to Sill Height: _____ Floor to Top of Window:_____

Multiple Window Width: _____ Height: _____

Type of Covering (draperies, blinds, etc.):_____

Supplied By:_____

Cost:_____ Date: _____

Measurements of Curtains, Blinds, Draperies: _____

Fabric & Cleaning Instructions: _____

Cleaned By: _____

Cost:_____ Date: _____

Notes:

Window 2 Size:

Measure glass area inside window to be covered.

Height: _____ Width: _____ Total Sq. Ft./M.: _____

Floor to Sill Height: _____ Floor to Top of Window:_____

Multiple Window Width: _____ Height: _____

Type of Covering (draperies, blinds, etc.):_____

Supplied By:_____

Cost:_____ Date: _____

Measurements of Curtains, Blinds, Draperies: _____

Fabric & Cleaning Instructions: _____

Cleaned By: _____

Cost:_____ Date: _____

Notes:

WALL FINISH

Wall Sizes:

North: _____ South: _____ East: _____ West: _____

Total Sq. Ft./M.: _____

1st. Type of Finish (paint, paper, etc.): _____

Supplied By:_____

Date: _____ Brand & Pattern:_____

Color & No: _____

Unit Cost: _____ No. of Units:_____ Total: _____

Installed By:_____

Date: _____ Cost:_____

Notes:

2nd. Type of Finish (woodwork, paneling, etc.): _____

Supplied By:_____

Date: _____ Brand & Pattern:_____

Color & No.:_____

Unit Cost: _____ No. of Units:_____ Total: _____

Installed By:_____

Date: _____ Cost:_____

Refinished By:_____

BEDROOM (CONTINUED)

Date: _____ Cost: _____

Notes:

CEILING FAN

Manufacturer & Model: _____

Supplied By: _____

Date: _____ Cost: _____

Warranty Period: _____

Installed By: _____

Date: _____ Cost: _____

Notes:

SAMPLES: PAINT, WALLPAPER, ETC.

attach wallpaper sample or daub paint sample here

FURNITURE / APPLIANCES

Item	Supplied By	Date	Cost	Warranty

BEDROOM NUMBER 3

FLOOR COVERING

Floor Size:

Measure from center of door to center of door, if any.

Width: _____ Length: _____ Total Sq. Ft./M.: _____

Type of Floor: (carpet, hardwood, etc.): _____

Supplied By: _____

Date: _____ Brand & Pattern: _____

Color & No.: _____

Unit Cost: _____ No. of Units: _____ Total: _____

Installed By: _____

Total: _____

Date: _____ Cost: _____

Serviced By: _____

Date 1: _____ Cost: _____

Date 2: _____ Cost: _____

Notes:

CEILING FINISH

Type of Finish (paint, spray texture, etc.): _____

Supplied By: _____

Date: _____ Brand & Pattern: _____

Color & No.: _____

Unit Cost: _____ No. of Units _____ Total: _____

Installed By: _____

BEDROOM (CONTINUED)

Date: _____ Cost:_____

Notes:

CURTAINS, BLINDS, DRAPERIES

Window 1 Size:

Measure glass area inside window to be covered.

Height: _____ Width: _____ Total Sq. Ft./M.: _____

Floor to Sill Height: _____ Floor to Top of Window:_____

Multiple Window Width: _____ Height: _____

Type of Covering (draperies, blinds, etc.):_____

Supplied By:_____

Cost:_____ Date: _____

Measurements of Curtains, Blinds, Draperies: _____

Fabric & Cleaning Instructions: _____

Cleaned By: _____

Cost:_____ Date: _____

Notes:

Window 2 Size:

Measure glass area inside window to be covered.

Height: _____ Width: _____ Total Sq. Ft./M.: _____

Floor to Sill Height: _____ Floor to Top of Window:_____

Multiple Window Width: _____ Height: _____

Type of Covering (draperies, blinds, etc.):_____

Supplied By:_____

Cost:_____ Date: _____

Measurements of Curtains, Blinds, Draperies: _____

Fabric & Cleaning Instructions: _____

Cleaned By: _____

Cost:_____ Date: _____

Notes:

WALL FINISH

Wall Sizes:

North: _____ South: _____ East: _____ West: _____

Total Sq. Ft./M.: _____

1st. Type of Finish (paint, paper, etc.): _____

Supplied By:_____

Date: _____ Brand & Pattern:_____

Color & No: _____

Unit Cost: _____ No. of Units:_____ Total: _____

Installed By:_____

Date: _____ Cost:_____

Notes:

2nd. Type of Finish (woodwork, paneling, etc.): _____

Supplied By:_____

Date: _____ Brand & Pattern:_____

Color & No.:_____

Unit Cost: _____ No. of Units:_____ Total: _____

Installed By:_____

Date: _____ Cost:_____

BEDROOM (continued)

Refinished By:_____

Date: _____ Cost:_____

Notes:

SAMPLES: PAINT, WALLPAPER, ETC.

attach wallpaper sample or daub paint sample here

FURNITURE / APPLIANCES

Item	Supplied By	Date	Cost	Warranty

BEDROOM NUMBER 4

FLOOR COVERING

Floor Size:

Measure from center of door to center of door, if any.

Width: _____ Length: _____ Total Sq. Ft./M.: _____

Type of Floor: (carpet, hardwood, etc.): _____

Supplied By: _____

Date: _____ Brand & Pattern: _____

Color & No.: _____

Unit Cost: _____ No. of Units: _____ Total: _____

Installed By: _____

Total: _____

Date: _____ Cost: _____

Serviced By: _____

Date 1: _____ Cost: _____

Date 2: _____ Cost: _____

Notes:

CEILING FINISH

Type of Finish (paint, spray texture, etc.): _____

Supplied By: _____

Date: _____ Brand & Pattern: _____

Color & No.: _____

Unit Cost: _____ No. of Units _____ Total: _____

Installed By: _____

BEDROOM (CONTINUED)

Date: _____ Cost:_____

Notes:

CURTAINS, BLINDS, DRAPERIES

Window 1 Size:

Measure glass area inside window to be covered.

Height: _____ Width: _____ Total Sq. Ft./M.: _____

Floor to Sill Height: _____ Floor to Top of Window:_____

Multiple Window Width: _____ Height: _____

Type of Covering (draperies, blinds, etc.):_____

Supplied By:_____

Cost:_____ Date: _____

Measurements of Curtains, Blinds, Draperies: _____

Fabric & Cleaning Instructions: _____

Cleaned By: _____

Cost:_____ Date: _____

Notes:

Window 2 Size:

Measure glass area inside window to be covered.

Height: _____ Width: _____ Total Sq. Ft./M.: _____

Floor to Sill Height: _____ Floor to Top of Window:_____

Multiple Window Width: _____ Height: _____

Type of Covering (draperies, blinds, etc.):_____

Supplied By:_____

Cost:_____ Date: _____

Measurements of Curtains, Blinds, Draperies: _____

Fabric & Cleaning Instructions: _____

Cleaned By: _____

Cost:_____ Date: _____

Notes:

WALL FINISH

Wall Sizes:

North: _____ South: _____ East: _____ West: _____

Total Sq. Ft./M.: _____

1st. Type of Finish (paint, paper, etc.): _____

Supplied By:_____

Date: _____ Brand & Pattern:_____

Color & No: _____

Unit Cost: _____ No. of Units:_____ Total: _____

Installed By:_____

Date: _____ Cost:_____

Notes:

2nd. Type of Finish (woodwork, paneling, etc.): _____

Supplied By:_____

Date: _____ Brand & Pattern:_____

Color & No.:_____

Unit Cost: _____ No. of Units:_____ Total: _____

Installed By:_____

BEDROOM (continued)

Date: _____ Cost: _____

Refinished By: _____

Date: _____ Cost: _____

Notes:

SAMPLES: PAINT, WALLPAPER, ETC.

attach wallpaper sample or daub paint sample here

FURNITURE / APPLIANCES

Item	Supplied By	Date	Cost	Warranty

BATHROOM NUMBER 1

FLOOR COVERING

Floor Size:

Measure from center of door to center of door, if any.

Width: _____ Length: _____ Total Sq. Ft./M.: _____

Type of Floor: (carpet, hardwood, etc.): _____

Supplied By: _____

Date: _____ Brand & Pattern: _____

Color & No.: _____

Unit Cost: _____ No. of Units: _____ Total: _____

Installed By: _____

Total: _____

Date: _____ Cost: _____

Serviced By: _____

Date 1: _____ Cost: _____

Date 2: _____ Cost: _____

Notes:

CEILING FINISH

Type of Finish (paint, spray texture, etc.): _____

Supplied By: _____

Date: _____ Brand & Pattern: _____

Color & No.: _____

Unit Cost: _____ No. of Units _____ Total: _____

Installed By: _____

BATHROOM (CONTINUED)

Date: _____ Cost:_____

Notes:

CURTAINS, BLINDS, DRAPERIES

Window Size:

Measure glass area inside window to be covered.

Height: _____ Width: _____ Total Sq. Ft./M.: _____

Floor to Sill Height: _____ Floor to Top of Window:_____

Multiple Window Width: _____ Height: _____

Type of Covering (draperies, blinds, etc.):_____

Supplied By:_____

Cost:_____ Date: _____

Measurements of Curtains, Blinds, Draperies: _____

Fabric & Cleaning Instructions: _____

Cleaned By: _____

Cost:_____ Date: _____

Notes:

WALL FINISH

Wall Sizes:

North: _____ South: _____ East: _____ West: _____

Total Sq. Ft./M.: _____

1st. Type of Finish (paint, paper, etc.): _____

Supplied By:_____

Date: _____ Brand & Pattern:_____

Color & No: _____

Unit Cost: _____ No. of Units:_____ Total: _____

Installed By:_____

Date: _____ Cost:_____

2nd. Type of Finish (woodwork, paneling, etc.): _____

Supplied By:_____

Date: _____ Brand & Pattern:_____

Color & No.:_____

Unit Cost: _____ No. of Units:_____ Total: _____

Installed By:_____

Date: _____ Cost:_____

Refinished By:_____

Date: _____ Cost:_____

Notes:

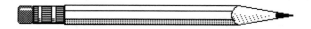

SAMPLES: PAINT, WALLPAPER, ETC.

attach wallpaper sample or daub paint sample here

BATHROOM NUMBER 2

FLOOR COVERING

Floor Size:

Measure from center of door to center of door, if any.

Width: _____ Length: _____ Total Sq. Ft./M.: _____

Type of Floor: (carpet, hardwood, etc.): _____

Supplied By: _____

Date: _____ Brand & Pattern: _____

Color & No.: _____

Unit Cost: _____ No. of Units: _____ Total: _____

Installed By: _____

Total: _____

Date: _____ Cost: _____

Serviced By: _____

Date 1: _____ Cost: _____

Date 2: _____ Cost: _____

Notes:

CEILING FINISH

Type of Finish (paint, spray texture, etc.): _____

Supplied By: _____

Date: _____ Brand & Pattern: _____

Color & No.: _____

Unit Cost: _____ No. of Units _____ Total: _____

Installed By: _____

Date: _____ Cost:_____

Notes:

CURTAINS, BLINDS, DRAPERIES

Window Size:

Measure glass area inside window to be covered.

Height: _____ Width: _____ Total Sq. Ft./M.: _____

Floor to Sill Height: _____ Floor to Top of Window:_____

Multiple Window Width: _____ Height: _____

Type of Covering (draperies, blinds, etc.):_____

Supplied By:_____

Cost:_____ Date: _____

Measurements of Curtains, Blinds, Draperies: _____

Fabric & Cleaning Instructions: _____

Cleaned By: _____

Cost:_____ Date: _____

Notes:

WALL FINISH

Wall Sizes:

North: _____ South: _____ East: _____ West: _____

Total Sq. Ft./M.: _____

1st. Type of Finish (paint, paper, etc.): _____

Supplied By:_____

Date: _____ Brand & Pattern:_____

Color & No: _____

BATHROOM (CONTINUED)

Unit Cost: _____ No. of Units: _____ Total: _____

Installed By: _____

Date: _____ Cost: _____

Notes:

2nd. Type of Finish (woodwork, paneling, etc.): _____

Supplied By: _____

Date: _____ Brand & Pattern: _____

Color & No.: _____

Unit Cost: _____ No. of Units: _____ Total: _____

Installed By: _____

Date: _____ Cost: _____

Refinished By: _____

Date: _____ Cost: _____

Notes:

SAMPLES: PAINT, WALLPAPER, ETC.

attach wallpaper sample or daub paint sample here

ELECTRICAL/WIRING

Suggestion: Sketch the layout of your fuse box. Label the fuses and identify the outlets and appliances they control.

ATTIC

Suggestion: Sketch the layout of your attic and list boxes and other items in storage, providing a location for each item.

MISCELLANEOUS ROOM 1

FLOOR COVERING

Floor Size:

Measure from center of door to center of door, if any.

Width: _____ Length: _____ Total Sq. Ft./M.: _____

Type of Floor: (carpet, hardwood, etc.): _____

Supplied By: _____

Date: _____ Brand & Pattern: _____

Color & No.: _____

Unit Cost: _____ No. of Units: _____ Total: _____

Installed By: _____

Total: _____

Date: _____ Cost: _____

Serviced By: _____

Date 1: _____ Cost: _____

Date 2: _____ Cost: _____

Notes:

CEILING FINISH

Type of Finish (paint, spray texture, etc.): _____

Supplied By: _____

Date: _____ Brand & Pattern: _____

Color & No.: _____

Unit Cost: _____ No. of Units _____ Total: _____

Installed By: _____

Date: _____ Cost:_____

Notes:

CURTAINS, BLINDS, DRAPERIES

Window 1 Size:

Measure glass area inside window to be covered.

Height: _____ Width: _____ Total Sq. Ft./M.: _____

Floor to Sill Height: _____ Floor to Top of Window:_____

Multiple Window Width: _____ Height: _____

Type of Covering (draperies, blinds, etc.): _____

Supplied By:_____

Cost:_____ Date: _____

Measurements of Curtains, Blinds, Draperies: _____

Fabric & Cleaning Instructions: _____

Cleaned By: _____

Cost:_____ Date: _____

Notes:

Window 2 Size:

Measure glass area inside window to be covered.

Height: _____ Width: _____ Total Sq. Ft./M.: _____

Floor to Sill Height: _____ Floor to Top of Window:_____

Multiple Window Width: _____ Height: _____

Type of Covering (draperies, blinds, etc.): _____

Supplied By:_____

MISCELLANEOUS ROOM (CONTINUED)

Cost:_____ Date: _____

Measurements of Curtains, Blinds, Draperies: _____

Fabric & Cleaning Instructions: _____

Cleaned By: _____

Cost:_____ Date: _____

Notes:

WALL FINISH

Wall Sizes:

North: _____ South: _____ East: _____ West: _____

Total Sq. Ft./M.: _____

1st. Type of Finish (paint, paper, etc.): _____

Supplied By:_____

Date: _____ Brand & Pattern:_____

Color & No: _____

Unit Cost: _____ No. of Units:_____ Total: _____

Installed By:_____

Date: _____ Cost:_____

Notes:

2nd. Type of Finish (woodwork, paneling, etc.): _____

Supplied By:_____

Date: _____ Brand & Pattern:_____

Color & No.:_____

Unit Cost: _____ No. of Units:_____ Total: _____

Installed By:_____

Date: _____ Cost: _____

Refinished By: _____

Date: _____ Cost: _____

Notes:

SAMPLES: PAINT, WALLPAPER, ETC.

attach wallpaper sample or daub paint sample here

FURNITURE / APPLIANCES

Item	Supplied By	Date	Cost	Warranty

MISCELLANEOUS ROOM 2

FLOOR COVERING

Floor Size:

Measure from center of door to center of door, if any.

Width: _____ Length: _____ Total Sq. Ft./M.: _____

Type of Floor: (carpet, hardwood, etc.): _____

Supplied By:_____

Date: _____ Brand & Pattern:_____

Color & No.:_____

Unit Cost: _____ No. of Units:_____ Total: _____

Installed By:_____

Total: _____

Date: _____ Cost:_____

Serviced By:_____

Date 1: _____ Cost:_____

Date 2: _____ Cost:_____

Notes:

CEILING FINISH

Type of Finish (paint, spray texture, etc.): _____

Supplied By:_____

Date: _____ Brand & Pattern:_____

Color & No.:_____

Unit Cost: _____ No. of Units _____ Total: _____

Installed By:_____

Date: _____ Cost:_____

Notes:

CEILING FAN

Manufacturer & Model:_____

Supplied By:_____

Date: _____ Cost:_____

Warranty Period:_____

Installed By:_____

Date: _____ Cost:_____

CURTAINS, BLINDS, DRAPERIES

Window 1 Size:

Measure glass area inside window to be covered.

Height: _____ Width: _____ Total Sq. Ft./M.: _____

Floor to Sill Height: _____ Floor to Top of Window:_____

Multiple Window Width: _____ Height: _____

Type of Covering (draperies, blinds, etc.):_____

Supplied By:_____

Cost:_____ Date: _____

Measurements of Curtains Blinds Draperies _____

Fabric & Cleaning Instructions: _____

Cleaned By: _____

Cost:_____ Date: _____

Notes:

MISCELLANEOUS ROOM (CONTINUED)

Window 2 Size: _____

Measure glass area inside window to be covered.

Height: _____ Width: _____ Total Sq. Ft./M.: _____

Floor to Sill Height: _____ Floor to Top of Window: _____

Multiple Window Width: _____ Height: _____

Type of Covering (draperies, blinds, etc.): _____

Supplied By: _____

Cost: _____ Date: _____

Measurements of Curtains Blinds Draperies _____

Fabric & Cleaning Instructions: _____

Cleaned By: _____

Cost: _____ Date: _____

Notes:

WALL FINISH

Wall Sizes:

North: _____ South: _____ East: _____ West: _____

Total Sq. Ft./M.: _____

1st. Type of Finish (paint, paper, etc.): _____

Supplied By: _____

Date: _____ Brand & Pattern: _____

Color & No: _____

Unit Cost: _____ No. of Units: _____ Total: _____

Installed By: _____

Date: _____ Cost: _____

Notes:

2nd. Type of Finish (woodwork, paneling, etc.): _____

Supplied By: _____

Date: _____ Brand & Pattern: _____

Color & No.: _____

Unit Cost: _____ No. of Units: _____ Total: _____

Installed By: _____

Date: _____ Cost: _____

Refinished By: _____

Date: _____ Cost: _____

Notes:

SAMPLES: PAINT, WALLPAPER, ETC.

attach wallpaper sample or daub paint sample here

FURNITURE / APPLIANCES

Item	Supplied By	Date	Cost	Warranty

STORAGE / CLOSETS

FLOOR COVERING

Floor Size:

Measure from center of door to center of door, if any.

Width: _____ Length: _____ Total Sq. Ft./M.: _____

Type of Floor: (carpet, hardwood, etc.): _____

Supplied By: _____

Date: _____ Brand & Pattern: _____

Color & No.: _____

Unit Cost: _____ No. of Units: _____ Total: _____

Installed By: _____

Total: _____

Date: _____ Cost: _____

Serviced By: _____

Date 1: _____ Cost: _____

Date 2: _____ Cost: _____

Notes:

CEILING FINISH

Type of Finish (paint, spray texture, etc.): _____

Supplied By: _____

Date: _____ Brand & Pattern: _____

Color & No.: _____

Unit Cost: _____ No. of Units _____ Total: _____

Installed By:_____

Date: _____ Cost:_____

Notes:

WALL FINISH

Wall Sizes:

North: _____ South: _____ East: _____ West: _____

Total Sq. Ft./M.: _____

1st. Type of Finish (paint, paper, etc.): _____

Supplied By:_____

Date: _____ Brand & Pattern:_____

Color & No: _____

Unit Cost: _____ No. of Units:_____ Total: _____

Installed By:_____

Date: _____ Cost:_____

Notes:

SAMPLES: PAINT, WALLPAPER, ETC.

attach wallpaper sample or daub paint sample here

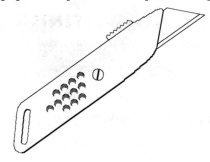

STORAGE / CLOSETS (continued)

Type of Wood (redwood, pine, etc.): _____

Supplied By: _____

Date: _____ Cost: _____

Sealed/Finished With: _____

No. Units: _____ Cost: _____

Brand, Color & No.: _____

Installed By: _____

Cost: _____

Refinished With: _____

Date: _____ Cost: _____

Notes:

Warning: Solid color oil or latex stains are unsuitable for use on floor surfaces.

DRIVEWAY

Type of Driveway (asphalt, concrete, etc.): _____

Sealant (brand, type, & no.): _____

Supplied By:_____

Date: _____ Unit Cost: _____

No. of Units:_____ Total: _____

Contractor:_____

Cost:_____

Notes:

Sealant (brand, type, & no.) _____

Supplied By:_____

Date: _____ Unit Cost: _____

No. of Units:_____ Total: _____

Contractor:_____

Cost:_____

Notes:

Sealant With (brand, type, & no.): _____

Supplied By:_____

Date: _____ Unit Cost: _____

No. of Units:_____ Total: _____

Contractor:_____

Cost:_____

FENCE

Type of Material (wood, metal, etc.) _____

Supplied By: _____

Sealant / Paint: _____ Date: _____

Brand, Color & No.: _____ Unit Cost: _____

Installed By: _____

Date: _____ Cost: _____

Refinished With: _____

Date: _____ Cost: _____

PATIO

Type of Material (wood, patio blocks, stone, cement, etc.) ___

Sealant: _____

Unit Cost: _____ Total Cost: _____

Installed By: _____

Date: _____ Cost: _____

Refinished With: _____

Date: _____ Cost: _____

Notes:

PORCH

Type of Materials: _____

Supplied By: _____

Brand / Specs: _____ Date: _____

Unit Cost: _____ Total Cost: _____

Contractor: _____

Date: _____ Cost: _____

Refinished With: _____

Date: _____ Cost: _____

DECK

Contractor: _____

Date(s): _____ Cost: _____

Type of Finish (paint, stain, etc.): _____

Supplied by: _____

Brand, Color, & No.: _____

Warranty Period: _____

GARAGE

FLOOR

Type of Floor (asphalt, concrete, etc.): _Concrete_

Sealant (brand, color, & no.): _____

Supplied by: _Chase-Pitken_

GARAGE (CONTINUED)

Date: _____ Unit Cost: _____

No. of Units: _____ Total: _____

Notes:

GUTTERS & DOWN SPOUTS

Type of Material (plastic, metal, etc.): _____

Supplied By: _____

Date: _____

Cost: _____ Warranty Period: _____

Installed By: _____

Date: _____

ROOF

Type of Roof (tile, shingle, etc.): _____

Weatherproofing: _____

Supplied By: _____

Brand, Color, & No.: _____

Unit Cost: _____ No. of Units: _____

Extras: _____

Cost: _____

Total: _____

Contractor: _____

Cost: _____

Date: _____

Warranty Period: _____

Total Job Cost: _____

SIDING

1st. Type of Siding (brick, stucco, etc.): _____

Supplied By: _____

Date: _____ Cost: _____

Brand, Color, & No.: _____

Warranty Period: _____

Contractor: _____

Cost: _____ Date: _____

Type of Finish (paint, stain, etc.): _____

Supplied By: _____

Date: _____

Brand, Color, & No.: _____

Warranty Period: _____

Unit Cost: _____ No. of Units: _____ Total: _____

Contractor: _____

Date: _____ Cost: _____

Notes:

2nd. Type of Siding (brick, stucco, etc.): _____

Supplied By: _____

Date: _____ Cost: _____

Brand, Color, & No.: _____

Warranty Period: _____

Contractor: _____

Date: _____ Cost: _____

Type of Finish (paint, stain, etc.): _____

Supplied By:_____

Brand, Color, & No.:_____

Date:_____ Warranty Period:_____

Unit Cost:_____ No. of Units:_____ Total:_____

Contractor:_____

Date:_____ Cost:_____

Notes:

TRIM

1st. Type of Trim (wood, aluminum, etc.):_____

Supplied By:_____

Date:_____ Cost:_____

Brand, Color, & No.:_____

Warranty Period:_____

Contractor:_____

Type of Finish (paint, stain, etc.):_____

Supplied By:_____

Brand, Color, & No.:_____ Date:_____

Warranty Period:_____

Unit Cost:_____ No. of Units:_____ Total:_____

Contractor:_____

Date:_____ Cost:_____

2nd. Type of Trim (wood, aluminum, etc.)_____

Supplied By:_____

Date: _____ Cost:_____

Brand, Color, & No.: _____

Warranty Period:_____

Contractor:_____

Date: _____ Cost:_____

Type of Finish (paint, stain, etc.): _____

Supplied By:_____

Date: _____

Brand, Color, & No.: _____

Warranty Period:_____

Unit Cost: _____ No. of Units:_____ Total: _____

Contractor:_____

Date: _____ Cost:_____

WALLS & CEILING

Type of Material (gypsum board, etc.): _____

Supplied By:_____

Date: _____

Unit Cost: _____ No. of Units:_____ Total: _____

Sealant (brand, color, & no.): _____

STORM WINDOWS

Supplied By:_____

Date: _____

Cost:_____ Warranty Period:_____

Contractor:_____

Cost:_____

Notes:

MAJOR TOOLS

Type of Tool (air compressor, bench grinder, etc.):_____

Supplied By:_____

Manufacturer:_____

Date: _____ Cost:_____

Model/Lot/Serial No.: _____

Authorized Service Center:_____

Warranty Period:_____

Type of Tool (air compressor, bench grinder, etc.):_____

Supplied By:_____

Manufacturer:_____

Date: _____ Cost:_____

Model/Lot/Serial No.: _____

Authorized Service Center:_____

Warranty Period:_____

ELECTRIC DOORS

Supplied By: _____

Date: _____ Cost: _____

Warranty Period: _____

Manufacturer & Model: _____

Serviced By: _____

Date 1: _____ Cost: _____

Date 2: _____ Cost: _____

TOOL SHED

Contractor: _____

Date(s) _____ Cost: _____

Type of Finish (paint, stain, etc.): _____

Supplied by: _____

Brand, Color, & No.: _____

Warranty Period: _____

Notes:

COOLING & HEATING

AIR CONDITIONER

Type of Unit (electric, natural gas, etc.): _____

Manufacturer & Model: _____ Efficiency: _____

Purchased From: _____

Date: _____ Cost: _____

Warranty Period: _____

Filter Type: _____

Size: _____

Cleaned/Serviced By: _____

Date No. 1: _____ Cost: _____

Date No. 2: _____ Cost: _____

Date No. 3: _____ Cost: _____

Date No. 4: _____ Cost: _____

Date No. 5: _____ Cost: _____

Date No. 6: _____ Cost: _____

Notes:

1st. FIREPLACE

Manufacturer & Model: _Heatilator_ _Nat. Gas_

Supplied By: _Miller Brick_

Date: _9-2004_ Cost: _____

Warranty Period: _____

Installed By: _____

Date: _____ Cost: _____

Chimney Cleaned By: _____

Date: _____ Cost: _____

Notes:

2ND. FIREPLACE

Manufacturer & Model: _____

Supplied By: _____

Date: _____ Cost: _____

Warranty Period: _____

Installed By: _____

Date: _____ Cost: _____

Chimney Cleaned By: _____

Date: _____ Cost: _____

Notes:

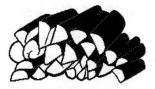

HEAT EXCHANGER / AIR FILTER

Manufacturer & Model: _____ Efficiency: _____

Supplied By: _____

Date: _____ Cost: _____

Warranty Period: _____

Filter Type: _____ Size: _____

Cleaned/Serviced By: _____

Date: _____ Cost: _____

HEATING AND COOLING (CONTINUED)
HEAT PUMP

Type of Unit (electric, fuel oil, etc.) _____

Manufacturer & Model: _____

Efficiency: _____

Supplied By: _____

Date: _____ Cost: _____

Warranty Period: _____

Filter Type: _____ Size: _____

Cleaned/Serviced By: _____

Date: _____ Cost: _____

Notes:

HEATING PLANT

1st. Type of Unit (electric, fuel oil, etc.): _____

Manufacturer & Model: _____ Efficiency: _____

Supplied By: _____

Date: _____ Cost: _____

Warranty Period: _____

Filter Type: _____ Size: _____

Humidifier: _____

Cleaned/Serviced By: _____

Date No. 1: _____ Cost: _____

Date No. 2: _____ Cost: _____

Notes:

WOOD STOVE

Manufacturer & Model: _____ Efficiency: _____

Supplied By: _____

Date: _____ Cost: _____

Warranty Period: _____

Chimney Cleaned By: _____

Date: _____ Cost: _____

Manufacturer & Model: _____ Efficiency: _____

Supplied By: _____

Date: _____ Cost: _____

Warranty Period: _____

Chimney Cleaned By: _____

Date: _____ Cost: _____

Notes:

TROMBE WALL, GREENHOUSE, OR ACTIVE SOLAR HEATING

Manufacturer & Model: _____

Supplied By: _____

Date: _____ Cost: _____

Warranty Period: _____

Installation Contractor: _____

Date: _____ Total Cost: _____

Warranty on Installation or Service Contract: _____

Notes:

INSULATION

ATTIC

Type of Insulation (fiberglass rolls, blown, etc.):

Cost: _____

Thickness: _____

R-Value Added: _____

Previous R-Value: _____

Aggregate R-Value: _____

Type of Vapor Barrier (6 mill poly, etc.): _____

Contractor: _____

Date: _____

Total Material Cost: _____ Total Cost: _____

Notes:

TYPE OF VENTING

Note: You should have one sq. ft. of free-flowing cross ventilation for every 150 sq. ft. of attic floor space. (Or one sq. meter to every 150 sq. meters). Soffit vents with screen covers can reduce air flow by up to 75%.

Under Eaves (Soffit) Sq. in./cm.: _____

Louvered Attic Vents Sq. in./cm.: _____

Low Pitch Slant Roof Vents Sq. in./cm.: _____

Turbines Sq. in./cm.: _____

Other: _____

Notes:

WALLS

1st. Type of Insulation (fiberglass, etc.): _____

Thickness: _____ R-Value: _____

Cost: _____

Aggregate R-Value: _____

Warranty Period: _____

Type of Vapor Barrier (6 mil. poly, etc.): _____

Contractor: _____

Date: _____

Total Material Cost: _____

Labor Cost _____ Total Cost: _____

Notes:

2nd. Type of Insulation (extruded polystyrene, etc.): _____

Thickness: _____ R-Value: _____

Cost: _____

Aggregate R-Value: _____

Warranty Period: _____

Type of Vapor Barrier (6 mill poly, etc.): _____

Contractor: _____

Date: _____ Total Material Cost: _____

Labor Cost _____ Total Cost: _____

Notes:

OTHER INSULATION

(rim joist, exterior foundation, etc.)

SECURITY AND SAFETY SYSTEMS

DOOR CHIMES

Name of System:_____

Supplied By:_____

Manufacturer:_____

Date: _____ Cost:_____

Model/Lot/Serial No.: _____

Authorized Service Center:_____

Warranty Period:_____

Notes:

(attach all receipts)

GARAGE DOOR OPENER

Name of System: _____

Supplied By: _____

Manufacturer: _____

Date: _____ Cost: _____

Model/Lot/Serial No.: _____

Authorized Service Center: _____

Warranty Period: _____

Notes:

(attach all receipts)

INTERCOM SYSTEM

Name of System: _____

Supplied By: _____

Manufacturer: _____

Date: _____ Cost: _____

Model/Lot/Serial No.: _____

Authorized Service Center: _____

Warranty Period: _____

Notes:

HOME SECURITY SYSTEM

Name of System:_____

Supplied By:_____

Manufacturer:_____

Date: _____ Cost:_____

Model/Lot/Serial No.: _____ Authorized Service Center:

Warranty Period:_____

Notes:

(attach all receipts)

SMOKE DETECTORS

Name of System:_____

Supplied By:_____

Manufacturer:_____

Date: _____ Cost:_____

Model/Lot/Serial No.: _____

Authorized Service Center:_____

Date 1 :Batteries Changed:_____

Date 2 :Batteries Changed:_____

Date 3 :Batteries Changed:_____

Date 4 :Batteries Changed:__ _____

Warranty Period:_____

It is good to make changing the batteries in the smoke detector part of an annual ritual, doing it every New Years Day, or on the First Day of Spring.

FIRE DETECTION SYSTEM

Name of System: _____

Supplied By: _____

Manufacturer: _____

Date: _____ Cost: _____

Model/Lot/Serial No.: _____

Authorized Service Center: _____

Warranty Period: _____

Notes:

VIDEO SECURITY SYSTEM

Name of System: _____

Supplied By: _____

Manufacturer: _____

Date: _____ Cost: _____

Model/Lot/Serial No.: _____

Authorized Service Center: _____

Warranty Period: _____

Notes:

TELEPHONES / FAX / ANSWERING MACHINES

Name of System:_____

Supplied By:_____ Manufacturer:_____

Date: _____ Cost:_____

Model/Lot/Serial No.: _____

Authorized Service Center:_____

Warranty Period:_____

Name of System:_____

Supplied By:_____ Manufacturer:_____

Date: _____ Cost:_____

Model/Lot/Serial No.: _____

Authorized Service Center:_____

Warranty Period:_____

Name of System:_____

Supplied By:_____ Manufacturer:_____

Date: _____ Cost:_____

Model/Lot/Serial No.: _____

Authorized Service Center:_____

Warranty Period:_____

Notes:

(attach all receipts)

THERMOSTAT / CLIMATE MONITORING

Name of System:_____

Supplied By:_____ Manufacturer:_____

Date: _____ Cost:_____

Model/Lot/Serial No.: _____

Authorized Service Center:_____

Warranty Period:_____

Notes:

(attach all receipts)

RADON TESTING & INFORMATION

Name of System:_____

Supplied By:_____ Manufacturer:_____

Date: _____ Cost:_____

Model/Lot/Serial No.: _____

Authorized Test Response Center(s): _____

_____

Phone:_____

Warranty Period:_____

Date of 1st Test: ___ Results:_____

Date of 2d Test:____ Results:_____

Notes:

WATER SYSTEMS

WELL

Drilling Contractor: _____

Date: _____ Cost: _____

Model/Lot/Serial No. of Pump: _____

Authorized Service Center/Repairman: _____

Warranty Period: _____

Notes:

WATER HEATER / SOLAR COLLECTOR

Name of System: _____

Supplied By: _____ Manufacturer: _____

Date: _____ Cost: _____

Model/Lot/Serial No.: _____

Authorized Service Center: _____

Warranty Period: _____

Installation Contractor: _____

Last Service Date: _____

Cost of Service: _____

Warranty on Installation or Service Contract: _____

Notes:

(attach all receipts)

WATER SOFTENER

Name of System:_____

Supplied By:_____ Manufacturer:_____

Date: _____ Cost:_____

Model/Lot/Serial No.: _____

Authorized Service Center:_____

Warranty Period:_____

Notes:

(attach all receipts)

WHIRLPOOL / HOT TUB / SAUNA / JACUZZI

Name of System:_____

Supplied By:_____ Manufacturer:_____

Date: _____ Cost:_____

Model/Lot/Serial No.: _____

Authorized Service Center:_____

Warranty Period:_____

Serviced By:

Date 1: _____ Cost: _____

Date 2: _____ Cost: _____

Date 3: _____ Cost: _____

SEWER / SEPTIC SYSTEM

Name of System:_____

Supplied By:_____ Manufacturer:_____

Date: _____ Cost:_____

Model/Lot/Serial No.: _____

Service:_____

Warranty Period:_____

Installation Contractor:_____

Last Service Date: _____

Cost of Service: _____

Warranty on Installation or Service Contract:_____

Notes:

(attach all receipts)

SUMP PUMP

Name of System:_____

Supplied By:_____

Manufacturer: _____

Date: _9-2004_____ Cost:_____

Model/Lot/Serial No.: _____

Authorized Service Center:_____

Warranty Period:_____

Notes:

(attach all receipts)

SPRINKLER SYSTEM

Name of System: _____

Supplied By: _____ Manufacturer: _____

Date: _____ Cost: _____

Model/Lot/Serial No.: _____

Service: _____

Warranty Period: _____

Installation Contractor: _____

Last Service Date: _____

Cost of Service: _____

Warranty on Installation or Service Contract: _____

Notes:

SWIMMING POOL

Name of System: _____

Supplied By: _____ Manufacturer: _____

Date: _____ Cost: _____

Model/Lot/Serial No.: _____

Service: _____

Warranty Period: _____

Installation Contractor: _____

Last Service Date: _____

Cost of Service: _____

Warranty on Installation or Service Contract: _____

Notes:

POOLHOUSE
ROOF

Type of Roof (tile, shingle, etc.): _____

Weatherproofing: _____

Supplied By: _____

Brand, Color, & No.: _____

Unit Cost: _____ No. of Units: _____

Extras: _____

Cost _____ Date:: _____

Reroofing Contractor: _____

Cost: _____ Date: _____

SIDING

1st. Type of Siding (brick, stucco, etc.): _____

Supplied By: _____

Cost _____ Date:: _____

Brand, Color, & No.: _____

Warranty Period: _____

Contractor: _____

Cost _____ Date:: _____

Type of Finish (paint, stain, etc.): _____

Supplied By: _____

Date: _____

Brand, Color, & No.: _____

Warranty Period: _____

Unit Cost: _____ No. of Units:_____ Total: _____

Contractor:_____

Cost _____ Date::_____

Notes:

WALLS & CEILING

Type of Material (gypsum board, etc.): _____

Supplied By:_____ Date: _____

Unit Cost: _____ No. of Units:_____ Total: _____

Sealant (brand, color, & no.): _____

Notes:

FLOOR

Type of Floor (asphalt, concrete, etc.): _____

Sealant (brand, color, & no.): _____

Supplied By:_____ Date: _____

Unit Cost: _____ No. of Units:_____ Total: _____

Notes:

BASEMENT

List anything that may be stored in your basement. If you maintain a wine cellar, provide an inventory, such as:

Chateau   *Vintage*   *Purchase Price*

_____

_____

_____

_____

_____

_____

_____

_____

_____

_____

_____

FLOOR COVERING

Floor Size:

Measure from center of door to center of door, if any.

Width: _____ Length: _____ Total Sq. Ft./M.: _____

Type of Floor: (carpet, hardwood, etc.): _____

Supplied By: _____

Date: _____ Brand & Pattern: _____

Color & No.: _____

Unit Cost: _____ No. of Units: _____ Total: _____

Installed By: _____

Total: _____

Date: _____ Cost: _____

Serviced By: _____

Date 1: _____ Cost: _____

Date 2: _____ Cost: _____

Notes:

CEILING FINISH

Type of Finish (paint, spray texture, etc.): _____

Supplied By: _____

Date: _____ Brand & Pattern: _____

Color & No.: _____

Unit Cost: _____ No. of Units _____ Total: _____

Installed By: _____

HOME OFFICE (CONTINUED)

Date: _____ Cost: _____

Notes:

CURTAINS, BLINDS, DRAPERIES

Window 1 Size:

Measure glass area inside window to be covered.

Height: _____ Width: _____ Total Sq. Ft./M.: _____

Floor to Sill Height: _____ Floor to Top of Window:_____

Multiple Window Width: _____ Height: _____

Type of Covering (draperies, blinds, etc.): _____

Supplied By: _____

Cost: _____ Date: _____

Measurements of Curtains, Blinds, Draperies: _____

Fabric & Cleaning Instructions: _____

Cleaned By: _____

Cost: _____ Date: _____

Notes:

Window 2 Size:

Measure glass area inside window to be covered.

Height: _____ Width: _____ Total Sq. Ft./M.: _____

Floor to Sill Height: _____ Floor to Top of Window: _____

Multiple Window Width: _____ Height: _____

Type of Covering (draperies, blinds, etc.): _____

Supplied By: _____

Cost: _____ Date: _____

Measurements of Curtains, Blinds, Draperies: _____

Fabric & Cleaning Instructions: _____

Cleaned By: _____

Cost: _____ Date: _____

Notes:

WALL FINISH

Wall Sizes:

North: _____ South: _____ East: _____ West: _____

Total Sq. Ft./M.: _____

1st. Type of Finish (paint, paper, etc.): _____

Supplied By: _____

Date: _____ Brand & Pattern: _____

Color & No: _____

Unit Cost: _____ No. of Units: _____ Total: _____

Installed By: _____

Date: _____ Cost: _____

Notes:

2nd. Type of Finish (woodwork, paneling, etc.): _____

Supplied By: _____

Date: _____ Brand & Pattern: _____

Color & No.: _____

Unit Cost: _____ No. of Units: _____ Total: _____

Installed By: _____

Date: _____ Cost: _____

Refinished By: _____

Date: _____ Cost: _____

CEILING FAN

Manufacturer & Model: _____

Supplied By: _____

Date: _____ Cost: _____

Warranty Period: _____

Installed By: _____

Date: _____ Cost: _____

Notes:

WALL SHELVES

Type of Finish (paint, varnish, etc.): _____

Supplied By: _____

Date: _____ Brand & Pattern: _____

Color & No.: _____

Unit Cost: _____ No. of Units _____ Total: _____

Installed By: _____

Date: _____ Cost: _____

SAMPLES: PAINT, WALLPAPER, ETC.
attach wallpaper sample or daub paint sample here

FURNITURE / APPLIANCES

Item	Supplied By	Date	Cost	Warranty

COMPUTERS / PERIPHERALS / MISCELLANEOUS EQUIPMENT

Desk top computer: _____

Model/Lot/Serial No.: _____

Supplied By: _____

Date: _____ Cost: _____

Authorized Service Center: _____

Warranty Period: _____

HOME OFFICE (CONTINUED)

Laptop/Message Pad: _____

Model/Lot/Serial No.: _____

Supplied By: _____

Date: _____ Cost: _____

Authorized Service Center: _____

Warranty Period: _____

Printer: _____

Model/Lot/Serial No.: _____

Supplied By: _____

Date: _____ Cost: _____

Authorized Service Center: _____

Warranty Period: _____

Other Peripherals (Fax Modem/CD-ROM/Hard Drives/DAT):

Item	Supplied By	Date	Cost	Warranty

ADDITIONAL HOME OFFICE
EQUIPMENT / REQUIREMENTS

Air Conditioning (Type of Unit): _____

Manufacturer & Model: _____ Efficiency: _____

Purchased From: _____

Date: _____ Cost: _____

Warranty Period: _____

Filter Type/Size: _____

Cleaned/Serviced By: _____

Date: _____ Cost: _____

Heating (Type of Unit): _____

Manufacturer & Model: _____ Efficiency: _____

Purchased From: _____

Date: _____ Cost: _____

Warranty Period: _____

Filter Type/Size: _____

Cleaned/Serviced By: _____

Date: _____ Cost: _____

Electrical Wiring and Outlets: _____

Supplied By: _____

Date: _____ Cost: _____

Warranty Period: _____

Installed By: _____

Date: _____ Cost: _____

HOME OFFICE (CONTINUED)

Phone Wiring and Jacks: _____

Supplied By: _____

Date: _____ Cost: _____

Installed By: _____

Date: _____ Cost: _____

Surge Protectors: _____

Model/Lot/Serial No.: _____

Supplied By: _____

Date: _____ Cost: _____

Authorized Service Center: _____

Warranty Period: _____

Lighting (lamps, fluorescent, etc): _____

Suppied By: _____

Date: _____ Cost: _____

Warranty Period: _____

Installed By: _____

Date: _____ Cost: _____

Cable Wiring and Jacks: _____

Date: _____ Cost: _____

Zoning contracts, applications, permits: _____

Date: _____ Cost: _____ Reason: _____

Date: _____ Cost: _____ Reason: _____

GAME ROOM

FLOOR COVERING

Floor Size:

Measure from center of door to center of door, if any.

Width: _____ Length: _____ Total Sq. Ft./M.: _____

Type of Floor: (carpet, hardwood, etc.): _____

Supplied By: _____

Date: _____ Brand & Pattern: _____

Color & No.: _____

Unit Cost: _____ No. of Units: _____ Total: _____

Installed By: _____

Total: _____

Date: _____ Cost: _____

Serviced By: _____

Date 1: _____ Cost: _____

Date 2: _____ Cost: _____

Notes:

CEILING FINISH

Type of Finish (paint, spray texture, etc.): _____

Supplied By: _____

Date: _____ Brand & Pattern: _____

Color & No.: _____

Unit Cost: _____ No. of Units _____ Total: _____

Installed By: _____

GAME ROOM (CONTINUED)

Date: _____ Cost: _____

Notes:

CURTAINS, BLINDS, DRAPERIES

Window 1 Size:

Measure glass area inside window to be covered.

Height: _____ Width: _____ Total Sq. Ft./M.: _____

Floor to Sill Height: _____ Floor to Top of Window:_____

Multiple Window Width: _____ Height: _____

Type of Covering (draperies, blinds, etc.): _____

Supplied By: _____

Cost: _____ Date: _____

Measurements of Curtains, Blinds, Draperies: _____

Fabric & Cleaning Instructions: _____

Cleaned By: _____

Cost: _____ Date: _____

Notes:

Window 2 Size:

Measure glass area inside window to be covered.

Height: _____ Width: _____ Total Sq. Ft./M.: _____

Floor to Sill Height: _____ Floor to Top of Window: _____

Multiple Window Width: _____ Height: _____

Type of Covering (draperies, blinds, etc.): _____

Supplied By: _____

Cost: _____ Date: _____

Measurements of Curtains, Blinds, Draperies: _____

Fabric & Cleaning Instructions: _____

Cleaned By: _____

Cost: _____ Date: _____

Notes:

WALL FINISH

Wall Sizes:

North: _____ South: _____ East: _____ West: _____

Total Sq. Ft./M.: _____

1st. Type of Finish (paint, paper, etc.): _____

Supplied By: _____

Date: _____ Brand & Pattern: _____

Color & No: _____

Unit Cost: _____ No. of Units: _____ Total: _____

Installed By: _____

Date: _____ Cost: _____

Notes:

2nd. Type of Finish (woodwork, paneling, etc.): _____

Supplied By: _____

Date: _____ Brand & Pattern: _____

Color & No.: _____

Unit Cost: _____ No. of Units: _____ Total: _____

Installed By: _____

Date: _____ Cost: _____

GAME ROOM (CONTINUED)

Refinished By: _____

Date: _____ Cost: _____

CEILING FAN

Manufacturer & Model: _____

Supplied By: _____

Date: _____ Cost: _____

Warranty Period: _____

Installed By: _____

Date: _____ Cost: _____

Notes:

SAMPLES: PAINT, WALLPAPER, ETC.
attach wallpaper sample or daub paint sample here

FURNITURE / APPLIANCES

Item	Supplied By	Date	Cost	Warranty

HOME ENTERTAINMENT ROOM

FLOOR COVERING

Floor Size:

Measure from center of door to center of door, if any.

Width: _____ Length: _____ Total Sq. Ft./M.: _____

Type of Floor: (carpet, hardwood, etc.): _____

Supplied By: _____

Date: _____ Brand & Pattern: _____

Color & No.: _____

Unit Cost: _____ No. of Units: _____ Total: _____

Installed By: _____

Total: _____

Date: _____ Cost: _____

Serviced By: _____

Date 1: _____ Cost: _____

Date 2: _____ Cost: _____

Notes:

CEILING FINISH

Type of Finish (paint, spray texture, etc.): _____

Supplied By: _____

Date: _____ Brand & Pattern: _____

Color & No.: _____

Unit Cost: _____ No. of Units _____ Total: _____

Installed By: _____

Date: _____ Cost: _____

Notes:

CURTAINS, BLINDS, DRAPERIES

Window 1 Size:

Measure glass area inside window to be covered.

Height: _____ Width: _____ Total Sq. Ft./M.: _____

Floor to Sill Height: _____ Floor to Top of Window:_____

Multiple Window Width: _____ Height: _____

Type of Covering (draperies, blinds, etc.): _____

Supplied By: _____

Cost: _____ Date: _____

Measurements of Curtains, Blinds, Draperies: _____

Fabric & Cleaning Instructions: _____

Cleaned By: _____

Cost: _____ Date: _____

Notes:

Window 2 Size:

Measure glass area inside window to be covered.

Height: _____ Width: _____ Total Sq. Ft./M.: _____

Floor to Sill Height: _____ Floor to Top of Window: _____

Multiple Window Width: _____ Height: _____

Type of Covering (draperies, blinds, etc.): _____

Supplied By: _____

Cost: _____ Date: _____

Measurements of Curtains, Blinds, Draperies: _____

Fabric & Cleaning Instructions: _____

Cleaned By: _____

Cost: _____ Date: _____

Notes:

WALL FINISH

Wall Sizes:

North: _____ South: _____ East: _____ West: _____

Total Sq. Ft./M.: _____

1st. Type of Finish (paint, paper, etc.): _____

Supplied By: _____

Date: _____ Brand & Pattern: _____

Color & No: _____

Unit Cost: _____ No. of Units: _____ Total: _____

Installed By: _____

Date: _____ Cost: _____

Notes:

2nd. Type of Finish (woodwork, paneling, etc.): _____

Supplied By: _____

Date: _____ Brand & Pattern: _____

Color & No.: _____

Unit Cost: _____ No. of Units: _____ Total: _____

Installed By: _____

Date: _____ Cost: _____

Refinished By: _____

Date: _____ Cost: _____

Notes:

CEILING FAN

Manufacturer & Model: _____

Supplied By: _____

Date: _____ Cost: _____

Warranty Period: _____

Installed By: _____

Date: _____ Cost: _____

SAMPLES: PAINT, WALLPAPER, ETC.

attach wallpaper sample or daub paint sample here

FURNITURE / APPLIANCES

Item	Supplied By	Date	Cost	Warranty

STEAM ROOM

FLOOR COVERING

Floor Size:

Measure from center of door to center of door, if any.

Width: _____ Length: _____ Total Sq. Ft./M.: _____

Type of Floor: (carpet, hardwood, etc.): _____

Supplied By: _____

Date: _____ Brand & Pattern: _____

Color & No.: _____

Unit Cost: _____ No. of Units: _____ Total: _____

Installed By: _____

Total: _____

Date: _____ Cost: _____

Serviced By: _____

Date 1: _____ Cost: _____

Date 2: _____ Cost: _____

Notes:

CEILING FINISH

Type of Finish (paint, spray texture, etc.): _____

Supplied By: _____

Date: _____ Brand & Pattern: _____

Color & No.: _____

Unit Cost: _____ No. of Units _____ Total: _____

Installed By: _____

STEAM ROOM (CONTINUED)

Date: _____ Cost: _____

Notes:

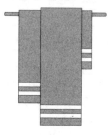

WALL FINISH

Wall Sizes:

North: _____ South: _____ East: _____ West: _____

Total Sq. Ft./M.: _____

1st. Type of Finish (paint, paper, etc.): _____

Supplied By: _____

Date: _____ Brand & Pattern: _____

Color & No: _____

Unit Cost: _____ No. of Units: _____ Total: _____

Installed By: _____

Date: _____ Cost: _____

Notes:

2nd. Type of Finish (woodwork, paneling, etc.): _____

Supplied By: _____

Date: _____ Brand & Pattern: _____

Color & No.: _____

Unit Cost: _____ No. of Units: _____ Total: _____

Installed By: _____

Date: _____ Cost: _____

Refinished By: _____

Date: _____ Cost: _____

Notes:

SAMPLES: PAINT, WALLPAPER, ETC.

attach wallpaper sample or daub paint sample here

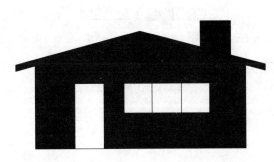

SUN ROOM

FLOOR COVERING

Floor Size:

Measure from center of door to center of door, if any.

Width: _____ Length: _____ Total Sq. Ft./M.: _____

Type of Floor: (carpet, hardwood, etc.): _____

Supplied By: _____

Date: _____ Brand & Pattern: _____

Color & No.: _____

Unit Cost: _____ No. of Units: _____ Total: _____

Installed By: _____

Total: _____

Date: _____ Cost: _____

Serviced By: _____

Date 1: _____ Cost: _____

Date 2: _____ Cost: _____

Notes:

CEILING FINISH

Type of Finish (paint, spray texture, etc.): _____

Supplied By: _____

Date: _____ Brand & Pattern: _____

Color & No.: _____

Unit Cost: _____ No. of Units _____ Total: _____

Installed By: _____

Date: _____ Cost: _____

Notes:

CURTAINS, BLINDS, DRAPERIES

Window 1 Size:

Measure glass area inside window to be covered.

Height: _____ Width: _____ Total Sq. Ft./M.: _____

Floor to Sill Height: _____ Floor to Top of Window:_____

Multiple Window Width: _____ Height: _____

Type of Covering (draperies, blinds, etc.): _____

Supplied By: _____

Cost: _____ Date: _____

Measurements of Curtains, Blinds, Draperies: _____

Fabric & Cleaning Instructions: _____

Cleaned By: _____

Cost: _____ Date: _____

Notes:

Window 2 Size:

Measure glass area inside window to be covered.

Height: _____ Width: _____ Total Sq. Ft./M.: _____

Floor to Sill Height: _____ Floor to Top of Window: _____

Multiple Window Width: _____ Height: _____

Type of Covering (draperies, blinds, etc.): _____

Supplied By: _____

Cost: _____ Date: _____

SUN ROOM (CONTINUED)

Measurements of Curtains, Blinds, Draperies: _____

Fabric & Cleaning Instructions: _____

Cleaned By: _____

Cost: _____ Date: _____

Notes:

WALL FINISH

Wall Sizes:

North: _____ South: _____ East: _____ West: _____

Total Sq. Ft./M.: _____

1st. Type of Finish (paint, paper, etc.): _____

Supplied By: _____

Date: _____ Brand & Pattern: _____

Color & No: _____

Unit Cost: _____ No. of Units: _____ Total: _____

Installed By: _____

Date: _____ Cost: _____

Notes:

2nd. Type of Finish (woodwork, paneling, etc.): _____

Supplied By: _____

Date: _____ Brand & Pattern: _____

Color & No.: _____

Unit Cost: _____ No. of Units: _____ Total: _____

Installed By: _____

Date: _____ Cost: _____

Refinished By: _____

Date: _____ Cost: _____

Notes:

SAMPLES: PAINT, WALLPAPER, ETC.

attach wallpaper sample or daub paint sample here

FURNITURE / APPLIANCES

Item	Supplied By	Date	Cost	Warranty

Index

PHONE NUMBERS

Type of Work	Name	Phone #
Air Conditioning		
Appliance Store		
Attorney		
Brick Company		
Cabinet Maker		
Carpenter		
Carpet Cleaner		
Carpet Store		
Drapery Cleaner		
Electrician		
Gardener		
General Handy Person		
Glazier		
Heating		
Insulator		
Lawn Maintenance		
Lumber Company		
Home Insurance		
Painter		
Paperer		
Plumber		
Sewer / Septic		
Sheetrocker		
Swimming Pool		
Tiler		
Trim Carpenter		
Window Company		

Notes:

The Home Owner's Diary